Monster Hunting

An Adventurer's Handbook

Alvin Nicholas

Zymurgy
Publishing

First published in Great Britain by Zymurgy Publishing in 2009.

Cover artwork Paul Goldsmith

10 9 8 7 6 5 4 3 2

A CIP catalogue record for this book is available from the British Library.

Printed and bound by Cromwell Press Group, U.K.

ISBN 978-1903506-33-2

Zymurgy Publishing
Newcastle upon Tyne

We urge you at all time to make yourself aware of and obey all laws, regulations and local bye laws and respect all rights, including the right of landowners, and all relevant laws protecting animals and plants and controlling the carrying and use of implements such as knives.

DISCLAIMER

The publisher and author disclaim any liability for accidents or injuries that may occur as a result of information given in this book. Neither the publisher or author accepts any responsibility for, or shall be liable for, any accident, loss or damage (including any consequential loss) that any reader may suffer after using the ideas, information, procedures or advice offered in this book.

It important and necessary to exercise common sense, particularly when fire, sharp objects and wild animals are involved, and follow at all times safety precautions and advice from responsible adults.

Treat wild animals with caution and observe from a respectful distance. Wild animals and their habitat should remain free from interference from 'Monster Hunters and Adventurers'.

Author

Alvin Nicholas earned BSc and MSc degrees at the University of Wales, Aberystwyth. He undertook field research on the elephants of Mount Elgon (a huge dormant volcano on the Kenya-Uganda border) and worked as a game ranger in South Africa. Whilst in Africa, Alvin was charged by elephants and shot at by rebels.

Back in Britain he is a qualified mountain leader and professional countryside ranger. He spends much of his spare time hunting for the Black Beast of the Moors in the mountains of South Wales.

Acknowledgements

Thanks to the many people in Africa and around the world who made this book possible. Special thanks go to Martin Ellis of Zymurgy Publishing and to Tamen Sitorus (Director, Komodo National Park) for his invaluable Komodo dragon advice.

Contents

WARNING! This is a wild, dangerous, untamed book that should be used with caution. Look out for the warning triangles.

Always heed the warning!

Raptor Head

How to Use This Book

You are about to train as a Beast Ranger, a monster hunter with extraordinary skills. This book is packed with tips and hints from wilderness adventurers, game rangers in Africa and top monster experts. You will learn essential skills to avoid Komodo dragon attacks and deal with Mongolian Death Worms. You will hunt for werewolves, battle Bigfoot and track dinosaurs. When you have completed your training, you will be ready for your quest.

Your Quest

Use your skills to investigate monsters, collect evidence and solve mysteries. Monsters generally fall into one of four categories:

1) Scary beasts

Scary beasts are 'normal' animals that scare people. Scary beasts are sometimes scary because they're dangerous. Sometimes, they're big and ugly (like giant catfish). Sometimes, they can be quite creepy (like hooting owls or a screaming vixen). You'll always find scary beasts in wildlife guidebooks.

2) Out–of–place animals

An out–of–place animal is an animal that is found in a place where it shouldn't be. For example, if a black panther from the Congo jungle escapes from a circus and decides to live on Bodmin Moor in Devon, it becomes an out–of–place animal. It shouldn't be there. The same would be true if you discovered a Nile crocodile in the pond in your back garden (unless you live in Africa). Since we're not used to seeing out–of–place animals, they're easily mistaken for cryptids.

3) Cryptids (undiscovered animals)

You won't find cryptids in modern wildlife guidebooks. Cryptids are animals that no one can prove exists. They are, however, still thought to be flesh–and–blood animals. Perhaps they have never been seen before, or maybe they are creatures that are supposed to be extinct. If they're discovered or rediscovered, they become 'normal' animals and are awarded a place in the guidebooks (mountain gorillas and Komodo dragons were once cryptids). If you can prove that a cryptid exists, you can expect to become quite famous, and if you discover a living dinosaur, you will become very famous indeed.

4) Supernatural monsters

Supernatural monsters seem to defy the known laws of nature. They appear from nowhere, suddenly disappear without a trace, float without wings and sometimes have eyes that glow. In many ways, they're similar to ghosts.

Note that monster categories 1–3 are flesh and blood animals. Here are a few tips to help you decide if you're dealing with flesh and blood or a beast from beyond:

Animals

* Always leave tracks and /or signs of their passing, even if they're difficult to find.
* Never defy the laws of nature. If they fly, they use wings. They can never vanish into thin air, or appear from nowhere (although it might seem like they can).
* Eyes might appear to glow when they reflect light (torch light, for example).

Supernatural Monsters

* Don't always leave a trace of their passing (although they might).
* Sometimes defy the known laws of nature. They fly without wings, vanish into thin air and appear from nowhere.
* Sometimes have self–luminous (glowing) eyes – often red. Why their eyes should glow and for what purpose is a mystery. Perhaps it's just to scare people!
* Could be alien life forms with extraordinary powers. Be sure to note such suspicions!

How to Find Fortune and Glory

Want to be a monster hunting mega star? Here are some ideas to make you rich, famous or both:

1. Prove the Loch Ness monster exists

Some really clear photos or camcorder footage would make you a household name, but samples of skin, hair, blood, a body or capturing the beast alive will make you rich through TV, film and book rights. If you don't live in Scotland, you could still hit the big time. Cash prizes have been offered for proof of the existence of Ogopogo, Champ, the Lliamna Lake Monster and others. See: *How to Solve Lake Monster Mysteries* and *How to Catch Lake Monsters* for tips.

Plessiorsaurous

2. Take a photo of Bigfoot

In 2008 a camera trap photo taken by Rick Jacobs of Pennsylvania inspired a $1 million 'prize challenge' for a genuine Bigfoot photo. Rick's photo seems to show a small ape–like creature, though sceptics claim it is a bear. Firm evidence of the existence of Bigfoot would bring fortune and glory on the same scale as discovering the Loch Ness Monster.

3. Find an animal thought to be extinct

Finding evidence of a living dinosaur (e.g. a recent egg or other evidence) would be astounding, since all the evidence suggests dinosaurs became extinct 65 million years ago. Try the remote jungles of the Congo Basin, the Amazon or Papua New Guinea. You never know. The coelacanth (pronounce see–la–kanth) is a weird–looking fish that was supposed to have become extinct with the dinosaurs. Until 1938 that is, when it was found alive and well.

You might try to find a creature that became extinct more recently. Take the Tasmanian tiger or thylacine. This hyena–like marsupial was thought to have become extinct on the Australian mainland thousands of years ago but survived until recent times on the island of Tasmania.

Tasmanian tigers had tiger–like stripes on their hinds and could open their jaws a full 120 degrees. They were no threat to humans, but were thought to be sheep killers.

The last wild tiger was shot in 1930 after it was discovered in a hen house. The last captive tiger died in Hobart Zoo in 1936. In 1986 the Tasmanian tiger was declared extinct – lost for all time, never to be seen again. All that remains are museum specimens and grainy film footage.

Perhaps all is not lost. Animals resembling Tasmanian tigers are reported on a regular basis in the Tasmanian wilderness as well as parts of western and eastern Australia. If there really are a few left in the wild it may be up to you to find them.

4. Find a Tyrannosuarus rex skeleton

The world's most famous dinosaur is an elusive beast. The largest and most complete skeleton ever found was christened 'Sue' (though no–one is sure if Sue is male or female). The 4 metre tall 13 metre long skeleton stands in The Field Museum, Chicago. Sue's skeleton is not a model – 'she' is the real thing. The discovery was controversial and led to arguments over the ownership and sale of important fossils.

Sue was found by and named after fossil hunter Sue Hendrickson after she found the skeleton sticking out of a sandstone cliff near Faith, South Dakota in 1990. Sue was eventually purchased by The Field Museum for a record–breaking $8.4 million.

Dakota is rich ground for dinosaur hunters. Equally incredible discoveries were made in 1999 and 2000: fossilised hadrosaur 'mummies' with internal organs and bones, still encased in their scaly skins!

5. Catch a $50,000 snake

You can claim a $50,000 'reward' from the Wildlife Conservation Society if you can catch a snake that is at least 30 feet (9.144 metres) long. It should be delivered alive and well with all necessary legal permits to the Bronx Zoo in New York City. See *How to Catch Giant Anacondas*.

6. Discover a new species

It might not make you a fortune, but discovering a new species will bring plenty of glory and a great deal of respect. You will also have the satisfaction of making a great contribution to science and wildlife conservation.

Even today there are many plants and animals that remain undiscovered on land and sea. About 1.75 million species are known to science out of an estimated 5–100 million species on the planet. This means there are between 3.25 million and 98.25 million species still to be discovered!

Spy Cams

Wildlife camera traps or 'trail cameras' are fantastic monster hunting tools. The most common types are digital cameras inside a tough case, adapted to take photos or capture video when they detect heat or movement. They are usually strapped or screwed to trees on game trails. Some use a flash and others have an invisible infrared setting to capture night shots (and cause less disturbance).

Basic models cost little more than the latest computer game. Whether you're in a remote jungle searching for undiscovered species, want to know what's roaming your woods or even your back garden, a camera trap can be left night and day, capturing images of whatever happens to pass by.

With a little help from an enthusiastic adult you can make a simple trap using a cheap disposable camera (see diagram). Set up a fishing line trip wire across a trail or tie some bait to the end of the line (the line and bait method can also be adapted to take photos of monster fish). Use an old belt to strap the device to a tree or some other convenient anchor.

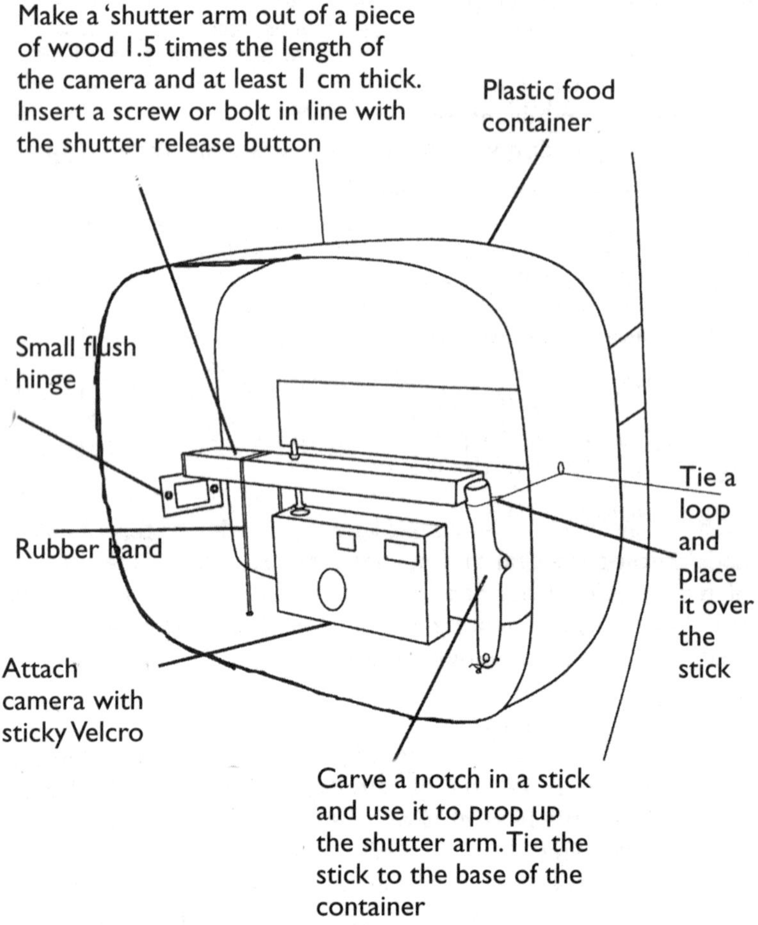

How to be a Real Life Indiana Jones

To help you choose your future career, the following jobs have been given marks out of ten for excitement, danger and the likelihood of being able to dress like Indiana Jones without being laughed at.

Museum Curator 1/10

Museum curators look after artefacts. They spend too much time indoors to score highly, but there might be the odd opportunity for adventure. You'll have to wait until closing time before you don your fedora and practice whip cracking.

Archaeologist 2/10

Don't imagine archaeologists lead a life of danger and adventure discovering powerful lost relicts. Archaeologists spend much of their time working in muddy holes, carefully scraping away the soil and getting excited about bits of old pottery. A lucky few do get to travel the world, visiting exotic places, but it's very rare. And if you think you'll carry a bullwhip and pistol you're going to be disappointed. Trowels and tape measures are the main tools of the trade!

Palaeontologist 3/10

Palaeontologists search for, discover and study the fossils of prehistoric plants and animals. As a palaeontologist, you could find yourself hunting for dinosaur eggs in the deserts of Mongolia. And as an expert on fossils, you would be a valued asset on expeditions in search of living dinosaurs.

Survival Expert 4/10

Teach others to survive in the wilderness. With all-round knowledge of the natural world, 'bushcraft' boffins make great monster hunters.

Volcanologist 5/10

Studying volcanoes and helping to save lives by predicting eruptions is certainly a worthwhile and exciting job. As a bonus, some volcanoes are said to be the home of weird creatures.

Bush Pilot 6/10

Super scary seat-of-your-pants flying and landing in remote wilderness areas. Bush pilots should be able to make repairs to their aeroplane and survive in hostile environments. What a job!

Mountain Guide 7/10

Get paid to take tourists on mountain climbing and walking trips. A great job if you're interested in mountain monsters like the Himalayan Yeti.

Safari Guide 8/10

Safari guides lead an exciting and adventurous lifestyle, leading tourists to view wildlife in remote and dangerous locations. Safari guides in Africa have similar skills to game rangers.

African Game Ranger 9/10

Game rangers look after wildlife in national parks and game reserves. One of the world's most interesting, exciting (and sometimes dangerous) jobs. You'll even wear a hat and learn to shoot a gun. Rangers in places like India, Alaska remote Australia and Indonesia also score highly.

Explorer-adventurer 10/10

The top spot goes to the explorer-adventurer – especially explorer-crytozoologists who lead or take part in expeditions to find cryptids (undiscovered animals). Many explorer-adventurers have regular paid jobs (like the jobs listed above) or make money by giving talks and writing books. Expect 'fortune and glory' if you can prove the existence of a living dinosaur.

How to Crack a Whip

You will need:

* **A nylon or leather whip**
* **Sunglasses or goggles**
* **A long–sleeved jacket and jeans**
* **A scarf to cover your ears and face**

The loud 'crack' from a whip is caused by a loop gaining speed until it breaks the sound barrier, causing a mini sonic boom. It sounds similar to a warning shot from a gun. In an extreme emergency in Africa, a crack from your whip might be enough to scare off a charging lion.

The main types of whips suitable for whip cracking are bullwhips, stock whips, cow whips and snake whips They range in length from about 1 metre to as long as 6 metres. You should start off with a whip that is about 1.8 metres long.

Most of the time, Indiana Jones uses a 3 metre leather bullwhip. He uses this to grab things, fend off baddies and swing like Tarzan. Grabbing (wrapping) is certainly possible with practice. However, some of the best fun to be had with a bullwhip is making very loud cracks, practising the many different moves and targeting empty plastic bottles.

RANGER TIP: The popper is a twisted piece of cord with a knot and a frayed end. If you buy a whip and it doesn't have one it probably won't crack, but you may get a few pops out of it if you add a 10 cm long piece of string or twine with a knot about an inch from the end.

Get Cracking

1. Put your safety gear on. Most beginners hit themselves with the whip whilst learning.

2. Grasp the knot (a bulge at the end of the handle) with your thumb on top, pointing foreword.

3. Lay the whip out in a straight line behind your whip hand.

4. With your arm by your side, swing up strongly, bending at the elbow in one smooth motion when your arm is pointing straight out in front of you. The whip should extend straight up into the air. Pause for a split second when your arm is vertical. The brief pause is to allow whip to drop down behind you. The exact timing will depend on the whip – the longer the whip the longer the pause.

5. Bring your arm forward in one smooth motion in like you're hammering a nail. Your arm should end up pointing straight in front of you and the whip should crack.

Practice makes perfect – and whip cracking requires lots of practice!

Whips can be dangerous. Always wear protective clothing and never crack a whip near people or animals

How to Pack for Adventure

This list will get you started on local monster hunting expeditions. You will need a bag – ether a small rucksack or preferably a super cool Indiana Jones–style shoulder bag (a World War II army issue gas mask bag was used in the films. You might find a similar bag in an army surplus store). An old tobacco tin can be used to safely store small, useful items: a small pencil and mini notepad, string for measuring giant snakes and making hides, emergency whistle, matches, a small mirror for reflecting sunlight (it will help you see into dark nooks and crannies), a magnifying glass, small plastic bags for collecting samples and a Swiss army type knife.

Here are the other essentials:

* Snacks and drinks.
* Binoculars.
* A camera. A disposable camera is a cheap and cheerful option. They can also be used to make trip wire camera traps.
* A torch. It should be bright enough to eyeshine (see *How to See Monster Eyeshine*).
* Head torches are the ideal all–round option but any good torch will do the job. Note: LED–type torches are long lasting but will not detect eyeshine.
* A baseplate compass. It will keep you on the right track. It might also 'detect' supernatural monsters since some people think mysterious forces make the needle spin.
* A map of the area in question.
* A guide to local wildlife. It is essential to know what's out there. If you don't, you won't be able to tell the difference between mystery monsters and local wildlife.
* A small first aid kit. See *First Aid for Beast Rangers* for how you might use it.

* Polarised sunglasses. They reduce glare and will help you spot monster fish and lake monsters below the water surface. They should also be used when whip cracking.
* A mobile phone for emergencies.
* This book. Keep it handy at all times.

Useful but not essential:

* A bullwhip. The loud 'crack' sounds like a gunshot and may scare away dangerous animals and aggressive monsters.
* A small brush (of the type found with a dustpan and brush). Used it to sweep sand or dust 'clean' to capture tracks in dry weather.
* Walkie–talkies to stay in touch on team adventures.

How to Stalk Monsters

Stalking is about getting close to something, whether it's a wild animal, an enemy or a monster, without being detected. Perhaps you want to take a photo of a monster, observe wild animals without them knowing or creep up on a friend and give them a fright. By combining tracking and stalking skills, you have a good chance of success.

Use camouflage

Adapt your clothing to the colour of the background. If you're in a jungle, wear dark green, if you're stalking at night, wear dark colours. Cover yourself in leaves and twigs to really blend in with the background.

Be like a cat

Cats are the world's best stalkers and you can learn a lot by watching them. Watch how they crouch and tread smoothly and carefully, with supreme balance and in complete silence. Observe how they stick to shadows and freeze at any hint of movement from their prey. You should do the same. Wear soft–soled shoes and walk on the ball of your foot, not your heels. Walk with your knees slightly bent but relaxed with your toes pointing forward. When you near your quarry, crawl on your hands and knees, keeping as low and quiet as possible. If at any point your quarry looks in your direction, FREEZE! Use anything to hide behind, remembering to watch from around the sides of your cover, not over the top as this will probably give you away.

Wait and see

The easiest way to stalk is to hide and wait. Climb up a tree or build a hide with branches and leaves (see *How to Build a Hide*). Be very quiet, still and patient and something will probably come your way.

The hunter's moon

Full moons are associated with werewolves, but can also be a great time to stalk (if you're brave enough to try), with just enough light to see, yet plenty of shadow to hide.

Stalk against the wind

Many animals have a powerful sense of smell and will pick up your scent at great distances, especially if it is carried towards them by the wind. Try to keep downwind as you stalk (with the wind blowing toward you). A strong and steady wind can have a double benefit for the stalker as it is much more difficult for the creature to hear you. To test the wind Kalahari Bushmen throw sand or dust into the air. If you come across an animal from the upwind side, you may be able to make a wide half–circle around it until the wind is in your face.

Avoid stalking too close to dangerous animals and monsters

How to Avoid Wild Beast Attacks

Your best defence against wild beast attacks is to remain undetected (see *How to Stalk Monsters*), but on occasions you will be spotted. The following information will not only help you survive an expedition, but will help you avoid the wrath of a wide range of monsters.

Why animals attack

Have you ever felt uncomfortable when someone has got too close to you? This is because they invaded your personal space, an area which is like an invisible bubble around your body. With dangerous animals, getting too close or invading the animal's personal space could be the last thing you ever do!

Animals have three zones within their personal space bubble. The zones are given a variety of different names, but in Africa they are known as the Alert Zone, the Warning Zone and the Attack Zone.

The zones in the diagram below are drawn from the point of view of the animal. In real life the size and shape of the zones change, depending on the particular species, weather conditions, whether it's a male or female, and of course, the nature of the individual since wild animals can be unpredictable.

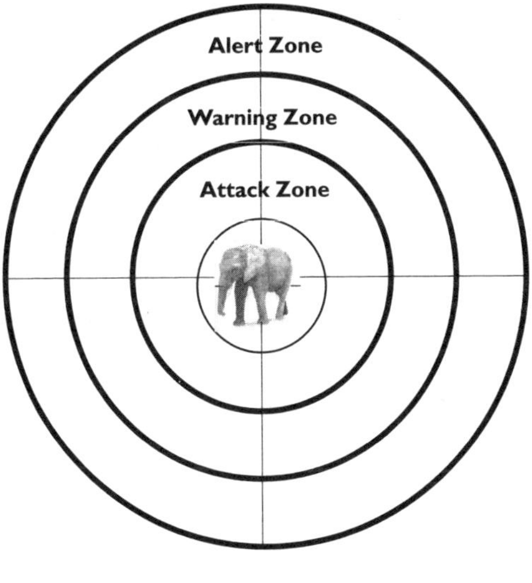

Heading for trouble

It is important to learn what happens when you approach a dangerous animal on foot and to discover some of the warning signs that mean 'back off!' We start off by assuming that the animal in question and the human spot each other at roughly the same time, since you can 'skip' zones by stumbling upon an animal or monster by accident, or by stalking dangerously close.

1. You are outside the Alert Zone, and it's 'business as usual'. The animal keeps an eye out for any sudden movements with an occasional glance. This is the safest place to be. Be sure that the animal has an easy escape route (animals will generally run away up wind, if possible) and above all, don't get any closer.

2. You continue to approach entering the Alert Zone. The animal freezes and watches you.

3. Moving in closer you enter the Warning Zone. The animal feels uncomfortable and either runs away or warns you that you are too close (growls, roars, snorts, claws the ground etc., depending on the particular species) All too often people fail to recognise these signs, whether it's an elk, a bison, bear or buffalo. If you don't back off at this point, you're asking for trouble.

4. You are completely bonkers and enter the Attack Zone. The animal feels so threatened it attacks (especially if it is cornered). Avoid the Attack Zone at all costs!

WARNING Testing this on a dangerous animal could provoke a fatal attack. If a dangerous animal reacts to your presence – you're too close!

RANGER TIP: Test the principle of 'personal space' on something small and harmless – squirrels in your local park, for example.

Stopping a charge

If the worst happens, try to keep your wits about you. Take advantage of trees, bushes, boulders and high ground. Make an unusual noise: crack your whip or beat a stick against a tree. If this doesn't work, wave your hands and shout loudly and aggressively. Game rangers will fire a warning shot if shouting fails (bear bangers of the type used in North America can be effective as well). Rangers will only shoot the animal dead as a very last resort when an attack is inevitable.

Man–eaters

Predatory attacks are different, since the animal wants to eat you! Thankfully they are very rare, but they usually require you to fight back in some way, depending on the species. Potential man–eaters on land include the big cats, crocodilians, wolves, bears, hyenas, Komodo dragons and giant snakes.

Lion

The most dangerous animal in Africa

Many game rangers will tell you that the cunning and unpredictable buffalo is the most dangerous of all the Big Five – elephant, buffalo, rhino, lion and leopard – traditionally the most dangerous animals to hunt on foot with guns, (though some ask why hippo and crocodile are not included). Apparently, a charging buffalo never stops (don't stand still if you're charged!).

Outside Africa, some of the buffalo's fierce instincts can still be observed in domesticated cattle. Most people are naturally wary of bulls, but cows can be equally dangerous if you get on the wrong side of them.

As with all animals, females with young should be treated with caution (NEVER get between a mother and a baby!) If you ever cross a field with cows and calves, give them plenty of space. If you have a dog with you, keep away. Cows with and without calves often see dogs as a threat – dangerous predators. If cows charge or stampede and you have a dog with you it is always best to let the dog go and make good your escape. The dog is fast, tough and stands a good chance. You might not!

How to Deal with Man–eating Lions

Lions strike fear into the heart, here are some facts about them.

* The African Lion is the second–biggest cat after the Siberian Tiger. Males stand 1.2 metres at the shoulder and can weigh over a quarter of a tonne.
* Most lions live in Africa, south of the Sahara Desert. A couple of hundred Asiatic lions survive in Gir National Park, India.
* Lions are the only cats that live in groups (called prides).
* Lions usually move away when they become aware of humans – unless, of course, they happen to be man–eaters.

Man eaters

The most famous man–eaters were the man–eaters of Tsavo. Over a period of nine months in 1898 two male lions killed as many as 135 workers constructing a bridge over the Tsavo River, Kenya (then known as British East Africa).

The lions sometimes dragged victims screaming from their beds. Chief engineer, Colonel John Henry Patterson wrote, "In the whole of my life I have encountered nothing more nerve–shaking than to hear the deep roars of these dreadful monsters growing gradually nearer and nearer, and to know that one or other of us was to be their victim before the morning dawned."

It was rumoured the beasts were 'werelions' and immune to bullets, but Patterson proved they were flesh and blood by shooting them. Patterson's incredible story was made into the film *The Ghost and the Darkness*.

More man–eating lions

The man–eating lions of the Njombe District of southern Tanzania were even deadlier than the man–eaters of Tsavo. It has been estimated that between 1932 and 1947 15 lions killed and ate up to 1500 people!

Warning signs

- * Look out for droppings and tracks, listen for roaring and laughing from hyenas. Zebra, wildebeest and giraffe may behave oddly when lions are around. They may be reluctant to drink from waterholes and stare at thick bushes.
- * Lions are night–hunters with excellent night vision. When camping at night in lion country, it's important to have a roaring fire and someone should stay awake to keep watch.
- * If you do encounter lions, stand still and slowly back away (downwind, if possible). If they become twitchy, stand still. Male lions usually avoid confrontation and run away. A female can be more of a problem (particularly if there are cubs around).
- * And man eating lions? Unfortunately, there will be no warning. Avoid areas with thick bush and long grass in regions that have a history of lion attacks. Man–eating behaviour is sometimes passed from generation to generation.

Attack!

A nervous lion will twitch its tail, but it's ears will remain upright. Back off while you can. An angry lion's ears will flatten and it will crouch low. Its tail may swish from side to side. It will cough and issue terrifying growls, before advancing towards you at a trot with its tail jerking up and down – finally breaking into a full charge.

Show no fear! If you run away the lion will instinctively chase and run you down. Stay still and as calm as possible, facing the lion and never taking your eyes off it. Hopefully it will stop a few metres short of you – at which point it may crouch flat on the ground roaring and snarling. Keep your nerve and it might suddenly turn then run off. There's a danger the lion will charge at you again so don't move away until you're sure it has left the area.

Lion

How to Build a Hide

Sometimes it is better to stay hidden and wait for monsters to come to you. A wildlife hide or screen will allow you to get closer to monsters so you can study their habits more closely or take a photo.

Whichever method you use, remember the following tips:

* Practice building hides in your garden before attempting to build them in the wilds.
* Spend some time observing your quarry and choose your spot carefully.
* When inside or behind a hide it is essential that you are quiet and still, otherwise you'll give yourself away. Get comfortable and be patient!
* Always build the hide downwind of your quarry
* A hide should be small, simple and natural looking. Use local vegetation to camouflage your hide so it blends in with the surroundings – the scruffier the better!
* The edge of a wood, or even better just inside the edge of a wood is an ideal site.
* Don't forget your camera and binoculars! A pencil and notebook will also come in handy.

Survival hide

This hide is based on the easy to build lean–to shelter. The main difference is to use it as a hide you will need small gaps in the foliage to see thorough. If you want to shelter from the elements you simply need to add more leaves, branches, grass etc. The advantage of this hide is that it looks completely natural.

1. Find two strong fairly straight sticks with Y– shaped ends for the uprights, each about 1.5 metres long.

2. Sharpen the non–forked ends and use a stone to knock them into the ground to a depth of about 0.3 metres, about 2 metres apart. If the ground is hard, lash together two tripods as an alternative.

3. Find a strong stick just over 2 metres long for a ridgepole.

4. Rest the ridgepole in the forks.

5. Lean 5–8 short roof poles on the ridgepole. Weave saplings in and out to secure the roof poles to the ridge pole or tie them together with string.

6. Weave leafy saplings in and out of the roof poles – not too thickly though; you need to be able to see through a gap!

Box hide

This hide looks like an expensive wildlife photography hide, but can be made with cheap gardening materials. As an alternative to garden canes, you can, of course, use straight thin sticks if you can find them.

You will need:

* **String**
* **Four 1.5 metre long garden canes for the uprights**
* **Four 1 metre long garden canes**
* **Garden netting (used by gardeners to stop birds and other critters helping themselves to fruit)**
* **Plenty of leaves, twigs etc. to camouflage the netting**
* **Scissors**

1. Push the long canes into the ground in a square; making sure that the distance between each upright is slightly less than the length of the shorter poles.

2. Tie the shorter canes to the top to form cross bars.

3. Drape the garden netting over the hide, remembering to leave a gap for the entrance at the back or side.

4. Camouflage the netting by inserting leaves, twigs, ferns, or whatever is available. Leave (get it?) a small gap in the vegetation for you to see through.

How to Track Monsters

Tracking is the oldest science. Practice whenever you get the chance and you'll soon be able to 'read' the ground like a book.

How to make a sand trap

A sand trap will tip the odds of finding tracks in your favour. Here's make one.

1. Dig a pit 5 cm deep and big enough to cover the area you expect to find some tracks (across a well used trail, for example).

2. Fill with sand, moisten with water and smooth the sand over.

3. Check daily. In dry dusty areas you can simply use a brush to sweep the area clear.

Look out for the tracks detailed on the following pages:

Collecting evidence

So you've found a Bigfoot track. It won't last long, and no one will ever believe you. So, you'll need to collect some evidence. If you have a camera, take some photos of the track and the surrounding area. Place a recognisable object near the track such as a pencil or better still a ruler to show scale. If the track is well defined you could make a plaster cast. Here's how:

1. Buy some plaster of Paris from your local craft shop.

2. Sweep away any dirt or debris from the track.

3. Make a circular collar out of cardboard to suit the size of the track and press down into the soil slightly.

4. Poor in the plaster of Paris until it is about an inch thick and leave to harden for 10–15 minutes. When you remove the cast you should find a 3D impression of the track on the bottom.

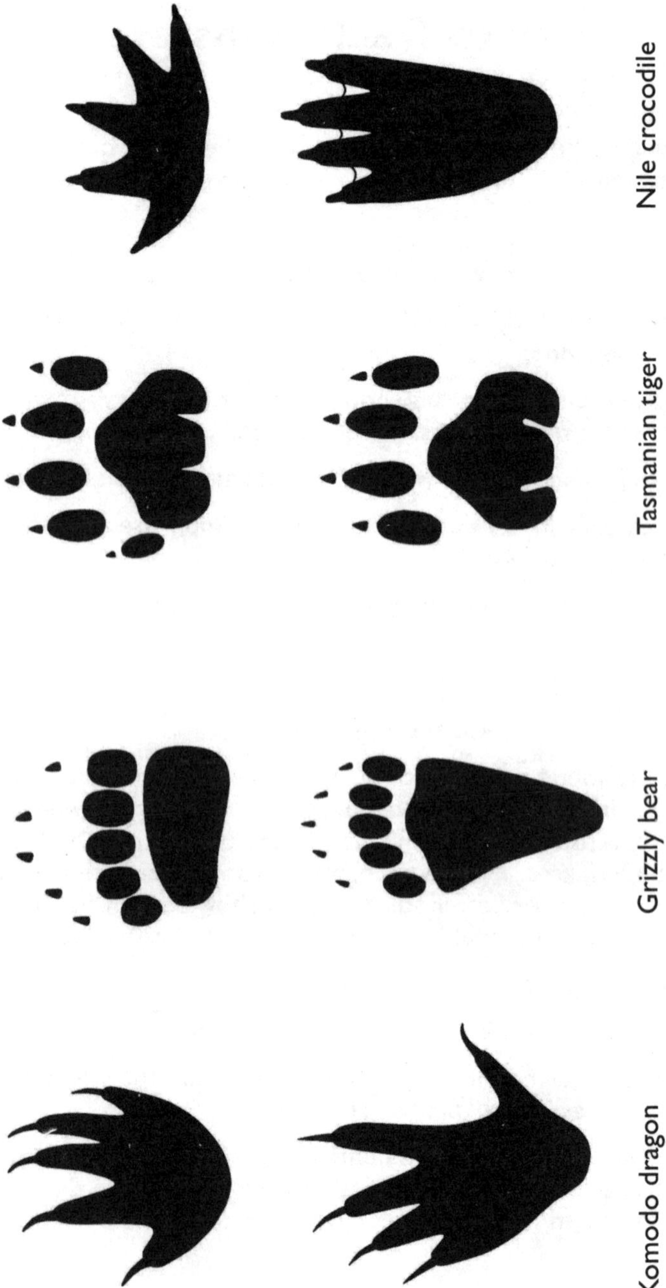
Komodo dragon
Grizzly bear
Tasmanian tiger
Nile crocodile

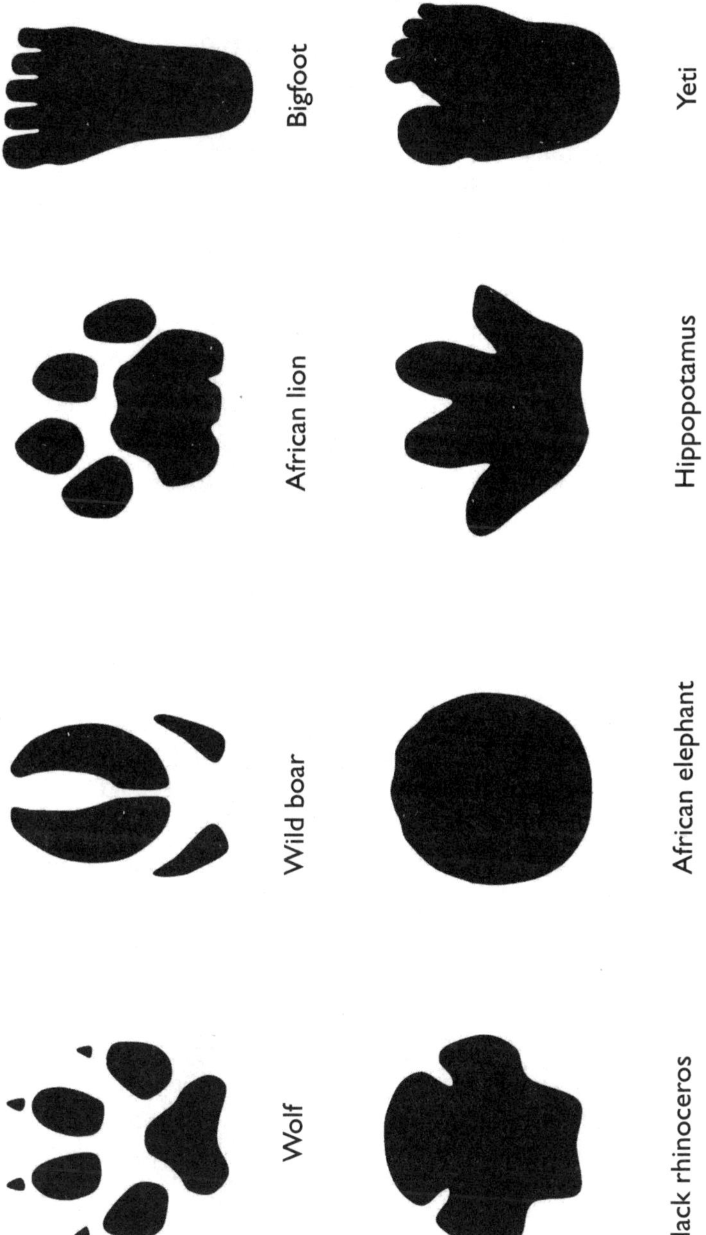
Bigfoot
Yeti
African lion
Hippopotamus
Wild boar
African elephant
Wolf
Black rhinoceros

Tracking tips

- * Tracks are most easily seen in snow, wet mud, sand around ponds and streams and in dry, dusty areas like dirt tracks.
- * Read up on local wildlife, their tracks and their habits. This will help you spot tracks that are unusual.
- * Track early in the morning or late in the day. The shadows cast by a low sun will make tracks easier to see. Tracking early has added advantages, because there is less chance sand traps will have been disturbed by humans and dogs, plus morning is the time when most animals are active.
- * Look for tracks a few metres ahead. Don't look down at your feet, as this will slow your progress.
- * Take care not to walk on the tracks (walk to the side). You may have to backtrack.
- * If you lose the trail, place a stick in the last visible track and start scouting around. Look in the direction of the last track and look for signs ahead such as bent grass, broken twigs and other small signs. Put yourself in the place of the creature you are tracking. Ask yourself, 'which way would I go?' Animals tend to take the easiest route of travel across a landscape (just like you and I – around boulders etc.), unless they are being pursued. This results in the creation of animal trails.
- * Alternatively, if you keep losing a trail make a tracking stick (see *How to Make a Monster Tracking Stick*).
- * If a track is clear and moist, it is recent. If it is dry, cracked or filled with bits of vegetation it is older. Study what happens to fresh tracks over periods of time and note your observations. This will help you judge the age of tracks more accurately.
- * Practice your tracking skills by tracking people. This has the advantage that you can practice almost anywhere– local parks, even towns.

How to Survive Bigfoot Attacks

For over 200 years Americans have reported seeing a creature that stands between 2 and 2.7 metres tall, weighs 270–360 kg, is covered head to foot with dark hair, has a massive barrel–like chest and very long arms – and, of course, very big feet. The North American Bigfoot hates dogs, has incredible strength and seems to be immune to bullets.

The wild and mountainous Pacific Northwest including Northwest California, Western Oregon, Washington State and British Columbia is prime Bigfoot country. Top spots include Bluff Creek, California (scene of a famous 1967 film showing what seems to be a Bigfoot) and the forested foothills of huge active volcanoes like Mount Shasta, Mount Rainer and Mount St Helens.

Bigfoot trap

In 1974 wildlife researchers constructed a Bigfoot trap in the Siskiyou National Forest, Oregon and bated it with animal carcasses. They caught only bears. A professional game capture team would probably choose to track Bigfoot creatures down and dart them – a method successfully used to capture great apes in the past.

Many countries have their own versions of Bigfoot. The Sumatran jungle is the home of the Orang-Pendek, while the Yeti or Abominable Snowman haunts the Himalayas of Nepal and Tibet. The Neanderthal–like Almasty inhabits central Asia and the Caucasus Mountains of Russia and Australia has the Yowie – a creature similar in appearance to the American Bigfoot, most often seen in the Blue Mountains of New South Wales.

The British Bigfoot is very odd indeed. Reported to have glowing red eyes, this creepy creature chases cars and often behaves in an aggressive manner. Recent reports of hairy man–beasts stalking the woods of Cannock Chase, England has led to speculation that bears or werewolves are on the loose!

Bigfoot attack!

In the summer of 1924 Fred Beck and four colleagues were prospecting for gold on the Muddy River 13 kilometres from Spirit Lake on Mount St Helens when they saw four Bigfoot creatures. One of the men – Marion Smith, fired at the creatures with a revolver. Although he thought that he hit it several times (including in the head), it just kept running. Fred Beck took a shot at one causing is to fall over a cliff. All night, the men found themselves under siege in their cabin as the creatures took their revenge, bombarding them with showers of rocks. The terrified men fired their guns at the ceiling as the creatures clambered onto the roof, trying to get in. The scene of the attack is still known as Ape Canyon.

Surviving Bigfoot attacks

Gorillas are super–strong primates native to Africa. Until Bigfoot is fully understood, your best chance of surviving an encounter is to treat it like the world's greatest ape. Here are some dos and don'ts if you find yourself in trouble:

- DON'T behave aggressively and DON'T throw sticks and stones.
- DON'T scream and above all, DON'T run away. As with big cats and bears, running away can lead to a full charge. If you are in a group, encourage everyone to stay together. Hold on to trees or one another to avoid being pulled to the ground.
- DO stay calm and quiet and DO stand your ground whilst avoiding direct eye contact (this could be seen as a challenge).

WARNING! Bigfoot country is often bear country. When in bear country, travel in groups, keep dogs on leads and carry bear spray or bear bangers in case of attacks. If you encounter a bear, stay calm. Speak to it so that it knows you're human and not on the menu. Don't run! Back away very slowly; making sure the bear has an escape route. Most defensive attacks are triggered when you get too close (100 metres is the recommended minimum distance). Lie on your stomach with legs apart to stop the bear flipping you over. Place your hands behind your neck. However, if the attack lasts more than a couple of minutes, or a bear has stalked you, assume a rare predatory attack (the bear wants to eat you). DO NOT PLAY DEAD. Fight back with all your might and try to escape.

How to See Monster Eyeshine

You will need:

* **A reasonably bright head torch or hand–held torch (non LED).**
* **Binoculars (optional, but useful).**
* **The ability to stay calm when confronted by 'glowing' eyes at night.**

Eyeshine spotting is great fun and can be a really useful monster identification tool. This amazing technique is used by safari guides and game rangers in Africa to spot animals like lion and buffalo at night, but it can be used anywhere in the world. Even if you don't spot a monster, you'll have a great time spotting secretive nocturnal wildlife.

Many animals have eyes that appear to glow in the dark when a light is shone at them. The effect is called eyeshine, and it is caused by a mirror–like layer in the eye called the tapetum (pronounced ta–PEE–tum). Most animals with strong eyeshine are nocturnal, and the tapetum helps them use the available light to see at night. Eyeshine can be seen in many mammals, reptiles, predatory fish, sharks, rays, frogs and wolf spiders.

RANGER TIP: Eyeshine can often be seen at great distances (sometimes over kilometres) even when the animal itself is not visible. If you're searching for something that is scary or dangerous, try using a more powerful torch or lamp (a red filter minimises disturbance). This way you can stay at a safe distance from your quarry.

Eyeshine colours to look out for include:

alligators & crocodiles – red

bear - red

big cats (most)– bright gold/green

Bigfoot–red – sometimes glowing

bogey beasts (hellhounds etc.) – glowing red

buffalo – bluish red

deer – bright orange/yellow/silver

dinosaurs – unknown – possibly red

dog family (fox, wolf etc.) – bright silver/gold /green

fruit bats – red

owls (most) – orange/red

owlman and mothman – red/glowing red

rabbits and hares – red

sheep – bluish green

warthog /bush pig/ wild boar – dull red/orange

Eyeshine colour will vary with the type of the light, distance and angle of the light – so look hard and long and get lots of practice identifying different species. In mammals,'bluish' eyeshine usually belongs to herbivores, and 'greenish' to carnivores, whose eyes appear especially green at a distance (beware of exceptions – some seals have blue eyeshine as did the Tasmanian tiger).

Don't forget to look for clues such as the distance between the eyes and the type of movement (if any). For example 'jerky' movements could indicate a small mammal like a rat.

Detecting night–time eyeshine

1. Remember, this technique won't work unless you hold the torch near your eyes. It is best to hold the torch on top of your head and look down the beam. Head torches are particularly useful because the light beam will be well placed just above your eyes to pick up eyeshine. Make sure the beam isn't too wide or too narrow (a medium focus works well in most situations).

2. The darker the night, the better. Carefully scan the surrounding area with your beam, watching for the eerie glow of eyeshine. Don't forget to scan tree branches and check water for possible aquatic monsters.

3. Try looking through binoculars whilst holding your torch directly below or above them. By lining–up the field of view with the end of the light beam you will improve your chances of seeing distant or difficult to see eyeshine such as those of small amphibians and reptiles.

4. Once you detect eyeshine, move in closer to your quarry (if you dare).

5. If when you remove the beam the eyes continue to glow, you may be dealing with a supernatural monster!

RANGER TIP: When you spot eyeshine, try mimicking the squeaks of a rabbit in distress by sucking the back of your hand. If the eyeshine belongs to a predator, it may come towards you!

Glowing red eyes

The creepy 'Owlman' highlights the importance of eyeshine. In 1976 several children and teenagers saw Owlman in the woods around the old church in the Cornish village of Mawman. On 3 July 1976 Sally Chapman and her friend were camping in the woods when they heard a hissing sound and saw Owlman. Sally said, "it was like a big owl with pointed ears, as big as a man. The eyes were red and glowing." It took off into the air and they saw its feet were "like pincers". ?

One theory is that Owlman is an out–of–place eagle owl. Native to mainland Europe, eagle owls are one of world's largest owl species and have been known to frighten people from time to time (with a wingspan of up to 1.8 metres, they're big enough to kill small deer and fox). A small population has become established in Britain and numbers are thought to be on the increase. When frightened, eagle owls hiss loudly and puff out their feathers. They have large orange eyes and bright red eyeshine. A clue, perhaps?

How to Track Dinosaurs

Tyrannosaurus rex

Dinosaurs died out at the end of the Cretaceous period, 65 million years ago. However, if numerous eyewitness accounts and tribal legends are to be believed, the vast rainforests of the Congo River basin in Central Africa (once described as the 'Heart of Darkness') are a 'lost world' a bit like *Jurassic Park*.

Mokèlé–mbèmbé ('one who stops the flow of rivers') is the most famous and well documented of the region's mystery creatures and the focus of many scientific expeditions. Reports suggest a dangerous and wary dinosaur–like beast living in the River Congo and the impenetrable swamps around Lake Tele, a large circular lake located deep within the forest.

Witnesses describe a creature about the size of a small elephant, with an extremely long neck and tail. (see *How to Solve Lake Monster Mysteries* for more on this amazing monster) Mokèlé–mbèmbé isn't the only monster. There have also been reports of:

* Stegosaur–like swamp–monsters with algae covered 'planks' growing out of their backs.
* A horned creature similar in appearance to a *Triceratops*.
* A flesh eating 12 metre long *Tyrannosaurus rex*–like monster called 'Kasai rex'
* A flying terror similar in appearance to a pterodactyl (see *How to Spot Time–travelling Pterosaurs*).

RANGER TIP: Forest elephant, lowland gorilla, forest buffalo and very large (possibly gigantic) crocodiles can be found in the Lake Tele area.

The Congo isn't the only place to hunt for living dinosaurs. Strange dinosaur–like creatures have also been spotted in:

* Papua New Guinea. Recent sightings include an '*Iguanodon*', said to stalk Umbungi Island, West New Britain.
* The Amazon. British explorer Lieutenant–Colonel Percy Harrison Fawcett (a 'real' Indiana Jones) saw what he described as a '*Diplodocus*' in the Amazon jungle in 1907.

So could the stories be true? The following information will help you track beasts that time forgot.

Dinosaur tracks

Dinosaur tracks are surprisingly common. It's an amazing feeling to *literally* follow in the footsteps of creatures that walked the earth millions of years ago. Like eggs and nests, dinosaur tracks are a direct connection with a time when the creature was *actually alive*.

A huge amount of information can be gleaned from dinosaur tracks (as can be gleaned from the tracks of living creatures). For example, palaeontologists can determine whether the dinosaur was running or walking, whether it was travelling on two legs or four, how fast it was travelling, whether it was alone or in a group and much more besides.

common dinosaur tracks

Sauropod tracks. Sauropods were plant–eating quadrupeds (dinosaurs that mostly stood on four legs) like *Brontosaurus* and *Brachiosaurus*. One of these beasts, the giraffe–like *Sauroposeidon* ('earthquake lizard–god') was one of the tallest dinosaurs ever. It could raise its head to about 18 metres, the height of four double–decker buses stacked one on top of the other. Super–giant sauropods like *Argentinosaurus* weighed more than ten fully–grown bull elephants, so it isn't surprising that tracks can be over a metre long and up to half a metre deep.

The rear tracks of sauropods can look a bit like giant bear tracks, and the front tracks are a bit like elephant tracks.

RANGER TIP: A series of tracks is called a trackway or trail. If the length between tracks is more than four times the length of a single track, the dinosaur was probably running.

Ornithopod tracks Ornithopods were broad–toed plant–eaters. Ornithopods like *Iguanodon* could probably switch between standing on two legs and four legs. Tracks are usually as wide as or wider than they are long, without claw marks.

Theropod tracks Theropods were narrow–toed bipedal carnivores – meat–eaters that mostly stood on two legs (like *Tyrannosaurus rex*). Tracks are usually longer than they are narrow, and may show evidence of claws at the ends of the toes.

How to Find Dinosaur Eggs

Brachiasauros

Like birds, dinosaurs laid eggs in nests. So if living dinosaurs really do exist in the remote jungles of Africa, South America and Southeast Asia they must be laying eggs. And if you're wondering how you might transport such an enormous egg to the nearest scientific research institution you need not worry. Most dinosaur eggs will fit comfortably into a small bag, because many dinosaur eggs weren't as big as you might imagine.

People have been finding dinosaur eggs for thousands of years, but they didn't know that they belonged to dinosaurs. The discovery of the first dinosaur eggs is usually credited to a series of expeditions to Mongolia in the 1920s and 30s led by American Roy Chapman Andrews. Andrews was an interesting chap, a real life Indiana Jones. He was a crack shot and always wore a battered ranger–style hat. He even had a 'monster' named after him: A wolf–like hoofed beast that grew bigger than a grizzly bear – the terrifying *Andrewsarchus*.

Palaeontologists have discovered that dinosaurs laid their eggs in nests. Some nests were bowl-shaped excavations – perhaps covered with vegetation. Some had mud rims. Sometimes the eggs were laid in long curving lines, or spiral patterns like this meat-eating theropod nest:

Nests could contain more than 20 eggs. Eggs were rounded or long and narrow with a hard shell like modern bird's eggs. Most (but not all) long and narrow eggs belonged to meat eating theropods, whereas rounded eggs generally belonged to non–theropods. And before you ask, no *Tyrannosaurus rex* eggs have ever been found, but they might look something like 43 cm long, 15 cm wide eggs from a large meat–eating dinosaur found in south–eastern China.

Naturally the big, plant–eating sauropod dinosaurs laid big eggs – up to 30 cm long and 25 cm wide in the case of *Hypselosaurus* eggs found in France in 1869. Although this would make a lot of scrambled egg, this is tiny when you consider sauropods were the largest land animals ever to have existed. So dinosaurs either grew very quickly or just grew and grew until they died.

Ostrich eggs (the biggest eggs of any living creature on the planet now) are of a comparable size to many dinosaur eggs, averaging 15 cm by 13 cm. However the egg of the extinct elephant bird measured 33 cm by 38 cm!

Egg size comparison

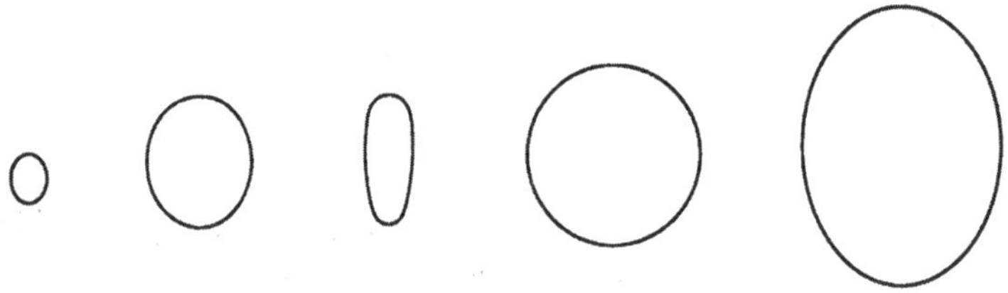

Chicken Ostrich Oviraptor[1] Sauropod elephant bird

What's inside?

The question everyone wants to know. The answer seems to be that often, not much, but now and again a fossilised egg contains a tiny skeleton that scientists can study and sometimes match to a particular type of dinosaur. Rarely, as in the case of dinosaur eggs found in the Patagonian desert in southern Argentina, patches of fossilised skin can be seen.

Dragon eggs

Reptiles other than dinosaurs also laid eggs. Pterosaurs (flying reptiles that lived at the same time as the dinosaurs), for example. Eggs have been found in China and Argentina. One of the eggs from China even contained the remains of a tiny pterosaur skeleton.

Lake monster eggs

Lake monster spotters who believe Nessie and others to be plesiosaurs, will be pleased to know experts think they might have laid eggs on sandy beaches a bit like turtles, but since no eggs have been found, no one can be completely sure.

Where to find dinosaur eggs

Dinosaur eggs have been found the world over. The Flaming Cliffs in the Gobi Desert, Mongolia, 'Egg Mountain' and 'Egg Island' in Montana are two of the most famous sites. Many eggs and eggshells (thousands in some cases) have been found in south–eastern China, Patagonia in southern Argentina, central India, north–eastern Spain and southeast France. The easiest way to see dinosaur eggs, however, is to visit the nearest museum to hold a collection!

[1] small man eating dinosaur

How to Make a Monster–tracking Stick

A tracking stick helps you see the next track. It does this by measuring stride length (the distance between the heels of two tracks). You can make tracking stick from a branch or a broom handle.

A metre is fine for most tracks, but remember that Bigfoot has an estimated stride length of 1–1.5 metres. *Tyrannosaurus rex* had an average stride length of 1.8 metres – increasing to a maximum of about 4.6 metres!

The Tracks in the diagram below belong to a *Tyrannosaurus rex*. In real life each track would be around 85 cm long and 70 cm wide.

Tracking stick

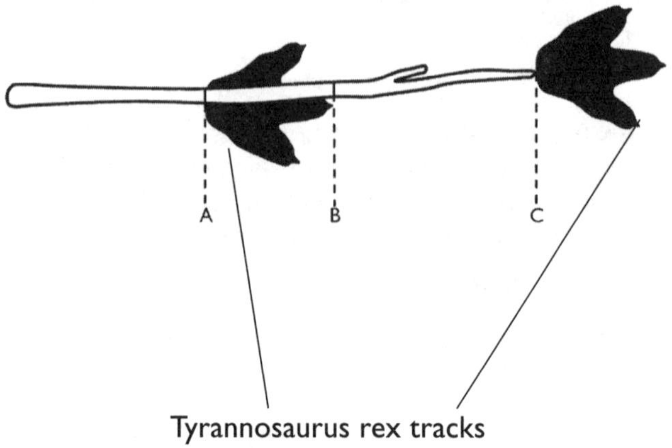

How to Track With a Tracking Stick

1. Find a clear series of tracks.

2. Place the tip of your stick (C) at the heel of a track, and carve a notch or place a rubber band at the heel of the previous track from the same foot (A).

3. Place a rubber band or carve a notch at the toe of the rear track (B) to measure its length (A-B).

4. If you lose site of tracks you are following, find the heel mark of the last visible track and hold your stick over it at point A. Move the stick in an arc whilst looking at the end of the stick for signs of disturbance that tell you that you have found the next track.

Sauropod

How to Deal with Deadly Spiders

Huge spiders are scary beasts indeed, but the most dangerous spiders are fairly small. Here are the deadliest:

Name: Brazilian wandering spider *(*banana spider*)*
Body length 3 cm
Danger Rating – 1st

The world's most dangerous spider, responsible for killing more people than any other. This super–aggressive critter is found in South and Central America and wanders the jungle floor at night. Brazilian wandering spiders have a nasty habit of turning up in supermarkets in crates of bananas. It rears up and sways from side to side when threatened.

Name: Sydney funnel–web

Body length: 1.5–3.5 cm
Danger Rating – 2nd

Annoying one of these large, aggressive Australian spiders would be a very bad idea. There are many species of funnel–web: the northern funnel–web and the Sydney funnel–web are the most dangerous. Although the northern funnel–web has the more powerful venom, the Sydney funnel–web lives close to people in Sydney and surrounding areas and is a greater threat to life. It rears up and displays vicious–looking fangs when threatened.

Name: Black widow spiders (*Latrodectus spp)*
Body length: 1 cm
Danger Rating – 3rd

Black widows are some of the world's most dangerous spiders, responsible for a number of deaths. With a distinctive red hourglass shape on the underside of the bulbous abdomen, the female is easily recognisable. Various species of black widow spider are found throughout the world, including continental Europe (other than the British Isles) and North America. In

Africa, they are known as button spiders, and in Australia they are known as redback spiders.

False black widow spiders can be found in Britain after arriving in bananas from abroad. They look a bit like true black widow spiders, but are far less dangerous to people.

Giant spiders

Found in parts of the Amazon and boasting a 30 cm leg span, the goliath bird–eating spider is thought to be the largest tarantula (although the pink–footed goliath is a strong contender for the title). A bite from the goliath's 2.5 cm long fangs would be extremely painful and might cause nausea and sweating, but shouldn't be fatal.

Desert horrors

One of the world's scariest 'spiders' isn't a spider at all, but a type of non–spider arachnid known as a solpugid, more commonly known as a camel spider. Looking like a cross between a scorpion and a spider, it is noted for its huge fangs. Camel spiders grow up to 13 cm long and can run at high speed over short distances. Experts say that rumours from the Middle East about huge camel spiders chasing people and inflicting horrific bite wounds are greatly exaggerated.

Avoiding spider bites

Spiders aren't interested in people and won't bite unless threatened. Leave them alone and they'll leave you alone. Tease a deadly spider and you're asking for trouble.

Use common sense in areas where deadly spiders are found. Check bedding before going to sleep, shake shoes and clothing before putting them on and don't go poking around wood piles, rock piles, and dark corners. See *First Aid for Beast Rangers* for spider bite treatment tips.

How to Spot Swamp Beasts

Visit the eerie swamps of the United States and you might see alligators, snakes and a host of amazing wild animals. And if you're 'lucky', you might spot something a little more unusual. If you thought the stinking, slimy *Creature from the Black Lagoon* was just a made–up movie monster, think again...

Swamp beast recognition

* Mainly found in North American swamps.
* Bipedal (they walk upright on two legs).
* Either hairy or scaly ranging in height from 1.2 - 3 metres.
* Striking red or orange eyeshine, sometimes described as 'glowing'.
* Mostly 3-toed tracks though sometimes 4. Be aware that alligator and bear tracks can easily be mistaken for swamp beast tracks.
* Swamp beasts can be highly aggressive and have a particular hatred of hunters.
* Swamp beasts never wash and they stink.

The Abominable Wookie

Honey Island Swamp in steamy Southeast Louisiana is virtually untouched by man – 650 square kilometres of wilderness that is considered to be one of the most pristine river swamp habitats in the United States. Take a guided boat tour and you might catch a glimpse of an American alligator, a beaver, a wild boar, a red wolf, a black bear or even a rare Florida panther. Oh yes, and you might even see the Honey Island Swamp Monster.

The 'thing' – simply called 'Wookie' by locals (the Wookie was a hairy alien in Star Wars) is described as a 2 metre tall, 230 kilogram Bigfoot-like beast covered in thick matted grey hair. The creature gives off a disgusting stench and has amber reptilian eyes.

Lizard Man attacks!

The Lizard Man of Scape Ore Swamp in South Carolina stands 2 metres tall, has green, scaly reptilian skin and glowing red eyes. In common with other swamp beasts it has three toes on each foot. It has 3 fingers on each hand and suckers on the ends of the fingers.

The creature has superhero levels of strength. Unfortunately, Lizard Man seems more interested in terrifying people than being a superhero! Late one night in 1988, 17 year-old Chris Davis stopped his car on the road next to Scape Ore Swamp to change a blown–out tyre. As he finished changing the tyre he saw a red–eyed, green skinned monster running towards him across a nearby field. He quickly got in his car and drove away but the creature gave chase, jumped onto the roof and tried to claw its way inside. Eventually Chris managed to shake the creature off. His car was left battered and scratched and the driver–side mirror had been wrenched off. Soon after, plaster casts were made of 35 cm, 3–toed tracks. In 2008 Lizard Man claimed another 'victim'. Scratches and damage to Bob and Dixie Rawson's car were blamed on the beast.

Bog Monster

Ferocious Fouke Monster

The 'Fouke Monster' (also known as the Monster of Boggey Creek) inhabits the woods and swamps around the town of Fouke, Arkansas. This 3–toed hairy biped has long matted hair, glowing red eyes and gives off a putrid stench in common with other swamp beasts. Reports of its height vary, with some claiming it stands around 1.2 metres tall but most claiming it is taller – 1.8–3 metres. The creature has a huge barrel–like chest and is known to make terrifying sounds at night – described by locals as a cross between a bellowing cow and a screaming panther (see *How to Identify Eerie Night–sounds*. The Fouke Monster seems untroubled by hunters' bullets and has evaded capture every time an attempt has been made to track the beast down.

Attack of the swamp beast

The Fouke Monster made the headlines when late one night in May 1971 it attacked the home of Bobby and Elizabeth Ford. At first, Elizabeth thought the creature was a bear as it reached through a window while she was sleeping on the sofa. Her husband Bobby and his brother returned from a hunting trip and chased the creature away only for it to return around midnight. It grabbed Bobby and threw him to the ground while he was standing on the porch. Fortunately he managed to escape the creature's clutches. Bobby reportedly needed hospital treatment and was deeply shocked by his experience. The usual 3–toed swamp beast footprints were found, and despite many sightings and a bounty on its head this aggressive creature remains at large. A film was made about the creature, called *The Legend of Boggey Creek*.

Stinking Skunk Apes

The four–toed Everglades Skunk Ape, Swamp Monkey or Stink Ape inhabits the incredible Everglades in Florida – a vast swampy wilderness that is one of the most important and spectacular wetlands on the planet. This 1.8–2 metre tall redhead stinks of rotten eggs. Well known to Indian tribes, Skunk Apes made headlines in 2000 when photos were taken of a large ape in a Florida garden. They show a creature similar in appearance to an orangutan with striking red eyeshine. The owner of the garden claimed the beast was stealing apples. The word 'orangutan' means 'person of the forest'. Thought to be the second most intelligent animal after humans, orangutans are large red–haired, fruit loving creatures found in the rainforests of Borneo and Sumatra. Could out–of–place orang–utans be roaming the Everglades? According to lifelong Skunk Ape researcher Dave Shealy, Big Cypress Swamp in Southern Florida is the best place to spot Skunk Apes (but be warned, this vast swamp is also home to venomous snakes, black bears, Florida panthers and alligators).

Hand from bog

How to Track the Black Beast of the Moors

Mystery big cats are reported throughout the world, from Australia to North America and Europe. The most famous of all are the 'black beasts' of Exmoor, Bodmin Moor and Dartmoor in the west of England, thought to be 'black panthers' released by their owners when a law named *The Dangerous Wild Animals Act* made it expensive to keep them.

The most common type of black panther in captivity is the black or melanistic leopard. In the wild, black leopards are most often found in dense jungles.

Whatever species of mystery big cat – whether it's a jaguar, mountain lion or one of the many other types, sound knowledge of tracking and dealing with African leopards provides the all-round skills to stay safe and solve mysteries.

Mountain cat

Leopard Facts

* African leopards are solitary, secretive and usually nocturnal (active at night). They are one of the most ferocious and cunning big cats.

* Leopards can weigh up to 60 kg and can kill prey 3–4 times heavier than themselves. According one study, they are the third most powerful big cats relative to their size (Cougar or Mountain Lion = 1st, Snow Leopard = 2nd, African Leopard = 3rd).

* The leopard is one of the world's most adaptable mammals – it can survive in many different environments – from mountains and semi–deserts to dense forest.

* On rare occasions leopards can become man–eaters – usually due to age, injury or because they have previously fed on human bodies. Most man–eating leopard accounts come from India, though there have been some recent incidents in Kruger National Park, South Africa. Lone children are most at risk, although bent over adults have also been attacked.

Signs of the Beast

* African leopards are most active in the early evening. They often travel along man–made roads and other trails.

* Leopards often use rocky terrain, scanning for prey from high vantage points.

* Leopard kills often have neck wounds (check the throat or back of neck). Bodies are usually dragged to cover or up into trees before feeding. Leopards usually eat from the groin and backside towards the head. They may return, so kill sites are good places to spot leopards.

* Leopards usually walk with their tails curled down and the end (tip) slightly up.

* Leopards sometimes use a particular tree to sharpen their claws. Look for distinctive claw marks. This behaviour can also be observed in domestic cats.

* Droppings are usually sausage–shaped with a tapered (pointed) end.

* Like other big cats, leopards have strong eyeshine; usually gold or green (See *How to See Monster Eyeshine*).

Catching the Beast

Expert 'game capture' teams catch big game in Africa, usually with the help of game rangers. Leopards are particularly dangerous to capture and will often attack if threatened. Firing a tranquilliser dart at a leopard can be risky, and getting close to leopards is difficult. The best method is to trap leopards in cage traps, perhaps set in trees since they are excellent climbers.

A cage trap is a strong metal cage with a sliding door at one end. The bait (such as fresh impala) is usually suspended from a wire attached to the door latch via pulleys and placed inside the trap. When the leopard tugs the bait, a latch holding up the door is released and it drops down behind the animal. A similar method involves a hinged floor. When the leopard steps inside the trap to get the bait the floor is pressed down, pulling a wire that releases the door catch. If the leopard escapes from the cage the trapper will be attacked (game capture teams will usually have guns). Once inside the cage the leopard is darted with a tranquilliser, which relaxes the animal so it can be safely handled.

WARNING The capture of dangerous animals should be left to qualified professionals.

* Leopards have a basic fear of humans and aren't dangerous if left alone. If teased, followed, wounded, cornered or suddenly disturbed they can be extremely dangerous. As with all dangerous animals, avoid females with young.

* The most common sound a leopard makes is a rasp, which sounds like wood being cut with a blunt saw. Leopards may growl and hiss if approached.

* Never run away from a leopard (or any other big cat). If you do it may trigger their predatory instincts.

Attack!

* If a leopard ambushes you, there will be no warning.
* If a leopard warns you by growling or hissing you should stop and retreat sideways, very slowly (don't turn your back to it, but don't stare at it). Don't throw anything at it and don't try to frighten it.
* If a leopard charges at you, nothing short of shooting it dead will stop it. It will charge very low to the ground and grab you with its powerful claws. It will usually try to kill you with a bite to the back of the head, neck or throat. It's a case of trying anything you can.
* Famous American naturalist Carl Akeley once wounded a leopard and unwisely returned the next day to track it. It flew at him, knocking his rifle out of his hand. In his account, he said, "she intended to sink her teeth into my throat and hold me tight in the grip of her jaws and forepaws while with her hind paws she dug at my stomach." Akeley somehow managed to kill the wounded leopard by choking it with his bare hands and crushing its ribs.
* A ranger in Kruger National Park was attacked by a leopard but managed to kill the leopard with his knife.

Leopard

WARNING The Beast of Exmoor, Dartmoor and Bodmin Moor may be just as dangerous as African leopards!

Use the illustrations opposite when tracking mystery big cats. Female leopard tracks are smaller. Mountain lion tracks are very similar to those of the leopard. You can see many of the features of leopard tracks in the smaller big cats as well as domestic cat tracks.

Big Dog or Big Cat?

1. Look at the overall shapes of the tracks. Leopard have a rounded track. Dog tracks are generally oval.

2. Most cats (other than cheetahs) have retractable claws that are rarely visible in tracks. Claw marks are usually visible in dog tracks.

3. The two front toes of the leopards track do not line up as they do in the dog track (A).

4. The front edge of the leopard's heel pad has two lobes (B). The dog track has a single lobe.

5. A game ranger trick to tell big dog tracks from big cat tracks is to draw an imaginary 'X' through the track (or use two blades of grass or two straight twigs). In cat tracks, the lines will go through the heel pad (C).

6. The back edge of the cat's heel pad has 3 even lobes (roughly in line). Dogs often have two lobes or the centre lobe is smaller (D).

Big Dog

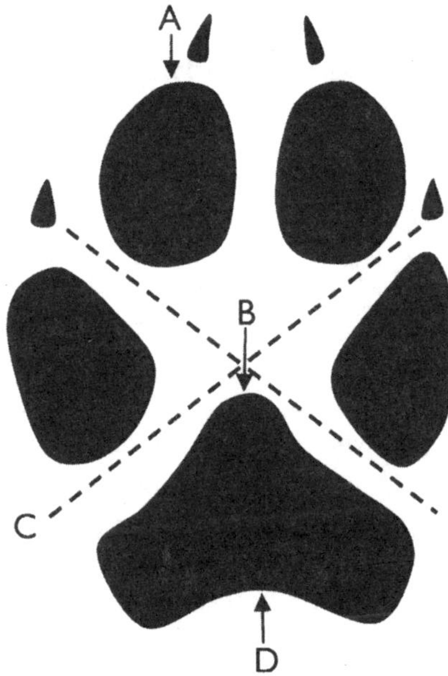

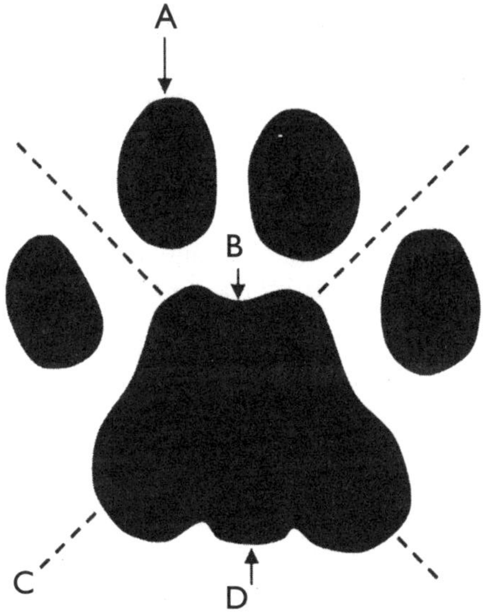

Big cat

Sabre–toothed Vampires?

Sabre-toothed cats with 30 cm long dagger–like canines survived until around 10,000 years ago in North and South America. Many hundred were trapped in the La-Brea Tar Pits in California and the History Museum of Los Angeles County has many complete specimens.

Smilodon could open its jaws an incredible 120 degrees, but it was a killing machine, not a bloodsucker. It used its extreme strength to wrestle prey to the ground and stabbed them through the throat with its vicious canines, severing the jugular vein. Death came quickly.

'Sabre–toothed cats' were reported in Colombia, Paraguay and Ecuador during the twentieth century. The sightings were probably of South America's largest big cat, the Jaguar.

How to Identify Eerie Night Sounds

Frightening screams have been heard in a nearby wood at night and there is talk of a 'savage beast' on the prowl. Here are the stop suspects:

Screaming fox

The long, wailing scream of a vixen (female) is probably the best–known eerie night–sound.Vixens scream to signal to males that they are ready to mate, you are most likely to hear the sound on mid-winter nights. Another common but less scary sound is a 'wow wow wow' bark.

Owls that screech

Barn owls are ghostly white birds found on farmland and in woodland. In flight, they are completely silent, but when they want to they can make quite a racket. Hearing the sudden rasping screech of a barn owl at night can be an unnerving experience. The owl makes the sound not only to mark its territory but also as an alarm call.

Screaming dear

Deer make all sorts of weird sounds, but the sounds made by sika deer are by far the weirdest. Sika deer are shy, secretive creatures native to east Asia but have been introduced to Britain, Ireland, mainland Europe, and north America. During the autumn rut (mating season) males make long, whistling cries and human–like screams (easily mistaken for distressed hikers). They are moist often heard at twilight and darkness in the early morning and early evening.

Screaming cats

Some types of cat can also 'scream'. The sound of domestic cats fighting at night are extremely weird, like cross between a tortured yowl and a crying baby. Although not often heard, the main call of the mountain lion (also known as the cougar, panther, or mountain screamer) is not a roar but a terrifying scream. It has been described as like the sound an 'unearthly vampire woman' (whatever that sounds like!)

Swamp beast!

It is possible that you are dealing with a swamp beast like the Fouke Monster (see *How to Spot Swamp Beasts*) or the screaming Murphysboro Mud Monster. This 2 metre tall blond–haired Bigfoot–like monster was seen, heard and tracked in the woods around Murphysboro, central Illinois in the summer of 1973. It had glowing red eyes and was always covered in mud.

RANGER TIP: To be sure of the identity of your screaming 'monster' you'll need to be familiar with sounds made by local wildlife. You can find many different wildlife sounds for free on the internet, but a wildlife sounds audio CD is well worth the investment.

How to Deal with Mega–hogs

The giant forest hog lives in the jungles of west and central Africa and can reach 2 metres in length, over one metre at the shoulder and weigh up to 275 kg. This, however, is nothing compared to the monster pigs of the swamps and woods of the southern United States.

Mega hogs

'Mega hogs' as they have become known came to the attention of monster hunters when a giant wild boar–domestic pig hybrid given the name 'Hogzilla' was shot and killed in Alapaha, Georgia in 2004. In 2005 the remains were dug up and examined by scientists who confirmed the beast was a monster. It weighed around 363 kg and was between 2.1 metres and 2.6 metres long.

Down in the woods

A huge wild boar supposedly destroyed trees and fences in the Forest of Dean, England in the early 1800s. Then in 1998 a wild boar 'the size of a cow' charged two terrified locals. Could the 'Beast of Dean' be the British Hogzilla?

The European wild boar was once widespread in Britain's woods, but was hunted to extinction in the late 1600s).

Wild boar farming in the 1980s brought the wild boar back to Britain's shores – and they have been busy escaping from captivity ever since. Once a wild boar escapes, its wild instincts return very quickly.

Since humans killed–off the wild boar's natural predators in Britain – wolves, lynx and bears – the population of wild boars has increased dramatically (incidentally, a 'bounty' was placed on wolves in the Forest of Dean in the Middle Ages as they were thought of as 'pests').

Today wild boar can be found in many woods throughout southern England, but one of the biggest populations can be found in the Forest of Dean! So it's just possible that a monster pig is lurking in the woods of deepest, darkest Britain.

Signs of the beast

Wild boar tracks are fairly easy to spot (see *How to Track Monsters*). Additional signs you should look for include:

* **Muddy puddles.** Pigs love wallowing in mud and wild boar are no exception.
* **Rubs.** Wild boars rub against trees after wallowing in mud to remove irritating parasites. Look out for worn bark and mud. Males also mark trees with their tusks.
* **Scrapes:** In the daytime wild boar nest in shallow pits in soil, sometime lined with leaves.
* **Rooting:** Wild boar root up the soil looking for food.
* Make no mistake, wild boar and wild boar – pig crossbreeds are dangerous animals.
* Keep your distance (see *How to Avoid Wild Beast Attacks*).
* Most of the time, wild boar are secretive and nocturnal so will run away before you see them. If you see wild boar move away calmly the way you came.
* If you come across a group of boar, the one that spots you may blow warning snorts to alert the others. Shout loudly and they should run away.
* Avoid sows with piglets. The mother will often give a warning snort, in which case it's time to leave.
* Avoid dense undergrowth in the spring as it provides cover for sows with piglets.
* Keep dogs on leads. Wild boar aren't keen on them!
* Remember that 'tame' wild boars could still be a threat, particularly if you have a dog with you. People who feed such animals are probably sealing their doom, as they will almost certainly become pests.
* Males attack using their tusks, while females lack tusks and use their teeth. The charge is likely to be sudden and if you can't get up a tree shout and make unusual noises to scare the animal away.

How to Build an Anti–monster Camp Fire

To build a fire, you will need to collect three types of fuel:

* **Tinder: dry grass, dead leaves, dry moss**
* **Kindling: thin twigs no thicker than a pencil, screwed up paper**
* **Fuel: thicker twigs, dry sticks and logs**

Use only dead, fallen wood. Hardwoods like oak, beech, holly, ash and birch burn evenly and slowly. They are good for long–lasting fires. Conifers burn quickly, spit, spark and give off lots of smoke.

The key to a good fire is to build it up gradually; starting off with the smallest (kindling) and ending with large fuel logs. The simple tepee fire provides lots of light – exactly what you need if lions, hyenas or monsters are on the prowl.

1. Make sure you have the landowner's permission to build a fire. Check fire regulations in national parks, forests, nature reserves and similar areas.

2. Clear a circle of about 3 metres in diameter down to bare soil. A circle of rocks around a shallow pit will help contain the fire and the ashes. If you are making a fire on green grass cut out a small square of turf and cut it to one side. You can replace it when you strike camp.

3. Put a bundle of tinder in the centre and gradually build out a triangular tepee shape around it. Make sure you leave an opening to light the tinder.

4. Add thicker twigs and sticks, maintaining the tepee shape.

5. Light the tinder at the centre to get the fire started.

Warning: Treat fire with respect. Build your fire well away from anything that could catch alight: tents, bushes, dry grass and overhanging tree branches. Always keep a container of water close by to put out your fire quickly, if necessary.

How to Deal with Werewolves

Torches at the ready, you and few friends set off to investigate reports of a howling beast in the local park. What could it be, and how will you deal with it? Here are four possibilities:

1 Howling Hound

Your 'monster' could be a howling hound. *The Hound of the Baskervilles* by Sir Arthur Conan Doyle is a famous tale about a dog mistaken for a monster. In the story, super sleuth Sherlock Holmes and his assistant Dr Watson travel to Dartmoor to solve a supernatural mystery. A demon–hound that has cursed the Baskerville family for generations has returned, threatening the life of the heir to Baskerville Hall, Sir Henry Baskerville. In the end the Hound of the Baskervilles turns out to be a half–staved dog, 'not a pure bloodhound and it was not a pure mastiff; but it appeared to be a combination of the two – gaunt, savage, and as large as a small lioness.'

Dealing with dogs Dogs can be dodgy. Domestic dogs attack more people every year than any other animal in this book, so it is definitely worth reading the following advice.

* If a dog approaches you, stand dead still and remain calm.
* Do not scream or run away.
* Do not turn your back on the dog.
* Make sure you know where the dog is but don't stare directly into its eyes. It may consider this to be a challenge
* If a dog approaches to sniff you, let it. It will probably realise you are not a threat and leave you alone. If you talk to the dog, speak in calm reassuring tones
* If it attacks, keep something between you and the dog (a bag, for example) or 'feed' it a stick.
* If you are knocked down by a dog, curl into a ball with your arms around your face, head and neck. Do not move or scream (play dead).

2 **Wild Wolf**

Why should a werewolf be scarier than a wolf? After all, isn't a werewolf merely *half* wolf? Wolves are killing machines – the very essence of wildness. Werewolves are wimps! Attacks on humans by wolves are very rare, but they do happen. Experts tell us they fall into three categories:

Mad wolves. The rabies virus attacks the brain and can make wolves want to bite anything in sight (although the victim isn't eaten). The deadly virus has a sinister mission. It 'wants' to infect other animals – or humans. The virus is concentrated in the rabid animal's saliva (drooling and foaming at the mouth are classic signs of the disease).

When the wolf bites another animal, rabies is passed on to the victim. In 1851 a rabid wolf bit 41 people in the Lorges Forest, France. 14 died of rabies. Rabid wolves may have inspired werewolf legends. A wolf or werewolf bites a man and he in turn becomes a blood–crazed werewolf. See the similarity?

3 **Hungry wolves.** Wolves usually go for the easiest meal option – kids! Don't be too worried. Predatory attacks (as they are known) are extremely rare. The Beast of Gévaudan, France was one of the most terrifying cases on record, Over one hundred people were said to have been killed and fifty injured by 2 or more unusually large wolves (thought to be werewolves at the time) over 3 years from 1764.

A much more recent attack in 2000 in Ice Bay, Alaska, involved two boys aged six and nine. They were playing at the back of their school when a snarling wolf came out of the forest. The boys turned and ran (a big mistake). One of the boys tripped over and was badly bitten. The wolf tried to carry the boy into the forest but dropped him. Lucky for him, a Labrador dog came to the rescue and the wolf slunk off into the forest. The boys father tracked–down and shot the wolf.

Frightened wolves (See *How to Avoid Wild Beast Attacks*). The easiest to avoid. Get too close, ignore the warnings and you might well be attacked.

Dealing with wolves

* Do not approach wolves, attempt to feed them or entice them closer. Wolves are cunningly clever and once they lose their fear of humans they become bolder and more dangerous.
* Don't allow a wolf to approach any closer than 100 metres.
* Never corner a wolf. Make sure it has an easy escape route.
* Wolves usually target wild animals with a weakness. If you are not 100% fit and confident in your manner they will know (they can even 'spot' if someone has a cold!)
* If a wolf acts aggressively (snarls and growls) DO NOT RUN AWAY. Make yourself as big as possible, waving your arms above your head. Make lots of noise and throw things.
* Maintain eye contact, back away slowly but never turn your back.

3 Bogey beast

Bogey beasts haunt lonely lanes, footpaths, bridges, crossroads, gateways, graveyards, ancient burial mounds, old manor houses and castles. Bogey beasts are thought to be evil spirits that take on a variety of frightening forms, most often phantom black dogs or 'hellhounds' with glowing red eyes. They are essentially boggarts and may take the form of other animals like horses, donkeys, pigs and even the occasional werewolf–like half human half animal hybrid.

How to become a werewolf

Traditionally it was thought that a human could be transformed into a werewolf by wearing a wolf skin or simply by sleeping outdoors when a full moon falls on a Friday.

Bogey beasts can be found throughout the world, but you are most likely to meet one in Britain. Here are a few examples:

* A phantom black dog rampaged through Bungay and Blythburgh churches in Suffolk during a powerful lightning storm in 1577. To this day, scorches can be seen on the door of Blythburgh Church – the claw marks of the beast.
* A werewolf–like monster patrols an ancient track near the village of Llysworney, South Wales It has the upper body of a human and the legs and body of a dog.
* The black dog of Winsford Hill in Exmoor National Park ambushes travellers then fades away until only glowing red eyes are left.

The Beast of Bray Road

A strange shape–shifting creature has been seen on many occasions in the US state of Wisconsin that fits the description of a 'traditional' werewolf. The Beast of Bray Road is usually seen at night by passing motorists. It looks like a bear standing on two legs, but has glowing yellow eyes, a long dog–like snout, protruding fangs and pointed ears.

Battling bogeys

If you encounter a bogey beast, you'll have to put your trust in old folklore books, which say that brandishing any object containing iron (a steel knife, for example) will cause it to vanish in an instant. You could try making a 'wizard staff' out of rowan wood (for extra fun, this could double as a tracking / Komodo dragon stick – see *How to Make a Monster Tracking Stick*, and *How to Deal with Komodo Dragons*). Rowan has been used for centuries to ward off witches, spooks and monsters, so it's definitely worth a try.

4 Lycanthrope. A Lycanthrope is a mentally ill person who believes that they transform into an animal. If you encounter such a person, alert the police for the sake of public safety.

How to Avoid Deadly Bogs

You are in hot pursuit of the Beast of Dartmoor. As you cross the windswept moors you imagine the newspaper headlines: 'Proof at last! Legendary beast caught on camera'. Suddenly you stumble into a mass of stinking, swampy bog vegetation. You are sinking fast and there is no help in sight. Should you be worried?

That depends. A bog or mire is a type of wet, marshy ground with specialised plants and peat (dead and decaying plants). Bogs develop in a number of soggy situations, but the most important bog–producing plant is sphagnum moss. When you step on sphagnum moss it will often feel like stepping onto a big green sponge.

Bog Avoidance

Bogs often support wildlife communities that are sensitive to disturbance. It is always best to avoid bogs (for the sake of the bog as well as your personal safety). Watch for water, green spongy sphagnum moss and bog grasses. If the ground becomes increasingly wet, retrace your steps. A walking stick can be handy to test the depth of bogs.

RANGER TIP You can get through bogs by 'bog hopping' from grassy tussock to grassy tussock, but you risk becoming trapped with a very good chance of ending up in the bog.

Bog Lights!

Whilst travelling across the moors on summer nights you might spot a flickering blue–green flame hovering just above the ground. Don't be tempted to follow such lights as they may be Jack O'Lanterns. They are thought to be caused by flaming bog gasses (though some say they are evil spirits, intent on luring travellers into trouble). Whatever the cause it will vanish as you approach and you'll find yourself ankle-deep in a bog!

If you get trapped

It is unusual to hear genuine stories about people getting sucked into a boggy oblivion. As many hill walkers will report, you are more likely to sink up to your knees and stop. Of course, even this could be a problem.

Deep bogs are like quicksand in that struggling will cause you to sink deeper. Don't panic! Remove your backpack and lie as flat as possible, spreading your weight on whatever you can get hold of. Crawl or swim on your stomach in the direction you came, since this is the only place you can be sure is firm ground.

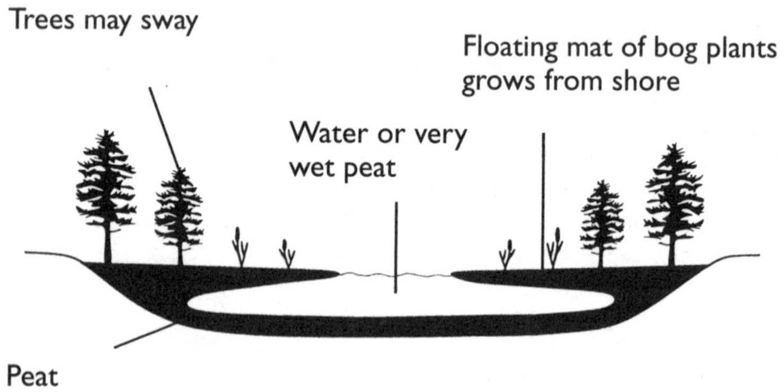

Quaking bogs

Avoid rare quaking bogs like the plague. If the ground wobbles and trees sway step back the way you came. If you find yourself trapped on a quaking bog remove any excess weight and spread your weight to avoid breaking through the crust. After all, you never know how deep the water beneath is and if you fall in it will be difficult to get out.

How to Deal with Super–rats

Rats are everywhere. These ravenous rodents thrive around humans, growing fat on food people throw away. And they're getting bigger. But even the biggest sewer rat can't match the cat–sized monster rats of New Guinea. Newly discovered *Mollomys* giant rats are five times bigger than sewer rats and according to scientists, have no fear of humans. Not that you're likely to meet one. They live in jungles so remote that have been hailed as real 'lost worlds'.

Dealing with rats

Rats have razor–sharp teeth and can carry a number of nasty diseases. You don't want to be bitten. Rats have been known to attack people, usually those unable to defend themselves (the very young, for example). You will often hear that a cornered rat is dangerous and will go for your throat. The first part is true (as with any cornered animal – see How *to Avoid Wild Beast Attacks*), but a rat is unlikely to attack your throat (most bites are to the hands).

Rat Tips

* Remember that rats are nocturnal. Avoid areas that are likely to have very high numbers of rats (old mines, for example), particularly after dark.
* If you come across a rat, give it an easy escape route and don't approach it.
* Don't try to deal with a rat yourself. Call a professional pest controller.
* If bitten, disinfect thoroughly and seek medical treatment.

How to Find Secret Passages, Tunnels and Chambers

Secret passages, tunnels and chambers are fairly common in Egyptian pyramids, castles, churches and old manor houses. They were used to confuse tomb raiders, help people to escape or hide in times of trouble, for smuggling or to conceal some other secret activity. If you suspect strange goings– on in your local castle, manor or millionaire's mansion here are some tips to help you solve the case.

Spot the difference

A secret passage is a concealed route to a secret chamber within a building or an escape route.

Secret tunnels are dug to connect two or more places – the most famous type being escape tunnels from castles and smugglers tunnels – still used in some parts of the world to this day.

Secret chambers are rooms that are hidden. A door or a panel may lead straight into the room or you may have to travel along a *secret passage* or *secret tunnel* to reach them.

Hiding places are small secret chambers used to hide in times of trouble.

Stashing places are small cunningly hidden storage areas, used for stashing valuables. Stashing places are commonly found in old beds.

Spy holes are used to watch people without being detected.

How to find them

Imagine you've travelled back in time to 17th Century England. You are a ruthless army captain in charge of a small group of government soldiers and you have arrived at a large manor house in search of a fugitive. It's fairly common for fugitives to escape or hide using secret passages and chambers. Here's what you do:

1. Lock up the owners. They may be able to pass on warnings or distract you from your task.

2. Carefully measure the outside walls and the rooms inside to calculate where gaps could conceal passages and chambers. Compare lower and upper rooms and pay particular attention to chimneys and fireplaces – by far the most common places to find secret passages and chambers.

3. 'Sound' the walls by tapping them with hammers, listening for hollow–sounding areas. Make holes in suspicious areas.

4. Remove floorboards, carpets, wooden wall panels, paintings and tapestries to uncover secret doors. Keep an eye out for spy–holes in the eyes of paintings and carvings.

5. Check for secret doors behind and beneath cupboards and other items of large furniture.

Castle monsters

With too many ghosts to mention, Glamis Castle, Scotland (pronounced 'glarms') is the most Hogwarts–like castle in existence. It is also the setting for the murder of King Duncan in Macbeth. A notorious tale concerns a mysterious secret chamber. According to one version, the eleventh earl of Strathmore had his deformed son locked up in the room, a child with an egg–shaped body, little or no neck, tiny arms and legs. He lived for more than one hundred years and was a closely guarded family secret. In 1904 the fourteenth earl of Strathmore, Claude Bowes–Lyon told a friend, "If you could only know the nature of the terrible secret, you would go down on your knees and thank God it is not yours." The family secret has never been revealed, so you will have to visit the castle yourself if you want to know more. While your there, count the windows. It is said that there are more on the outside than rooms on the inside!

Top Tips:

* Longer tunnels and passages may be revealed through draughts and strange noises caused by the wind (may be mistaken for ghosts).
* Sometimes secret passages were booby–trapped and intruders would fall into a deep pit or dungeon after stepping on a false floor.
* A cunning mechanism may engage a hidden door. Pay particular attention to the library. Secret doors in bookshelves are fairly easy to construct and may be opened by a book attached to pulley mechanism. In Balfour Castle, Scotland. A secret passage is located behind a set of false bookshelves, leading to the drawing room. When the owners of the castle had unwanted visitors they would make good their escape!
* In modern houses belonging to eccentric millionaires a hidden switch might engage a door opening mechanism.

Caves and mines

Caves, tunnels and abandoned mines may be home to bears, big cats and the occasional Bigfoot. It goes without saying that you should NEVER enter a cave, tunnel or mine without a knowledgeable professional guide and the correct safety equipment. It's simply not worth the risk.

The best way to investigate is to watch the entrance and wait – from a distance!

How to Use Telescopes and Binoculars

The Beast Ranger should always keep a pair of binoculars handy. They are fantastic for all–round monster spotting and other outdoor adventures. Here's how they work:

* The two halves of a pair of binoculars are basically two small telescopes joined together by a hinge. Having two small telescopes instead of one increases the amount you can see (the field of view).
* Adjust the binoculars in and out at the hinge to suit the distance between your eyes.
* A central focus wheel adjusts the focus in both halves of the binoculars at the same time. However, since most people have different strengths of vision in each eye there is a further instrument to allow you to match this difference, a rotating eyepiece called the diopter.
* The diopter can usually to be found on the right–hand eyepiece. If this is the case close your right eye and focus on a distant object with your left eye using only the central focus wheel. Then close your left eye and rotate the diopter until the object is in focus. The binoculars are now set for your eyes.
* When using binoculars, keep them around your neck until you identify a target area. Without taking your eyes off the target, raise the binoculars up to your eyes without moving your head.

Choosing binoculars

When choosing binoculars, note the magnification (power) and the diameter of the objective lens (the wide end). This will be described using two numbers, as in '10 x 50' or '8 x 25'. The first of the two numbers refers to the magnification – '10x' means an object will appear 10 times larger than with the naked eye. However, high magnification can make binoculars more difficult to use, since it is difficult to hold steady. The second number is very important. It refers to the diameter of the objective lens. A bigger objective lens gathers more light and can be used in lower light conditions – handy for twilight monster hunters! Choose something like a 7 x 50 to for good all–round monster hunting performance.

Spotting scopes

If you've found something with your binoculars, you may want to take a closer look. A spotting scope is a portable telescope that is designed for terrestrial use as opposed to stargazing (spotting scopes can be used for both, however). Like binoculars they will have an eyepiece and a focus wheel, but unlike binoculars you will almost certainly require a tripod. Spotting scopes are usually more powerful than binoculars, so it is possible to zoom in closer. Some will allow you to attach a camera to take long–range photos.

How to Spot Time–travelling Pterosaurs

Pteranodon

You are investigating reports of a flying beast at a local beauty spot. Several witnesses swear they saw a 'pterodactyl'. Are you dealing with a monster or a case of mistaken identity? Use this guide to uncover the truth.

'Terror' dactyls

Pterosaurs or 'pterodactyls' were a group of flying reptiles that sometimes grew to be the size of small aeroplanes. They ruled the skies at the same time dinosaurs ruled the earth and suffered the same fate. Pterosaurs became extinct 65 million years ago.

But that hasn't stopped people seeing them!

* Terrifying pterosaur–like monsters have been spotted in southern Texas – particularly around the Rio Grande River valley. In 1976 three schoolteachers were 'buzzed' by a creature so large its wings cast a dark shadow as it swooped over their car.
* A pterosaur fossil was found in 1971 at Big Bend National Park – which also happens to be in Texas. And it wasn't just any pterosaur. With a wingspan of up to 12 metres it was the largest known pterosaur ever to have existed, named after the Aztec winged serpent god, *Quetzalcoatlus*.
* Pterosaur fossils have also been found near 2100 metre Mount Pilatus in Switzerland. The mountain is famous for sightings of bat–winged 'dragons'. Apparently, they were once a common sight!

Snallygaster!

Not an insult, but the name of a bloodsucking dragon or pterosaur–like monster said to inhabit the Blue Ridge Mountains near Braddock Heights, Maryland, United States. The Snallygaster is described as a huge half bird, half reptile beast with vicious teeth and a metallic–looking beak. In 1909 a Snallygaster was reported to make a sound 'like a locomotive whistle'.

The Smithsonian Institution in Washington DC offered a reward to anyone who could kill the beast. Former US President Theodore Roosevelt considered postponing his famous African safari so that he could hunt it down personally!

Jurassic Jungles

Perhaps President Roosevelt could have got some pterosaur target practice in Africa while he was on safari. Deep within swamps of Zimbabwe, Kenya, Zambia, Angola and the Congo (where many 'dinosaurs' have been reported), Kongamato rules the skies. Kongamato means 'breaker of boats'. The beast has bat–like wings, a wingspan of 1.2 –2.1 metres and a crocodile's body! As you might have guessed, locals claim it attacks canoes.

Across the ocean in South America pterosaur–like monsters have been spotted in the Amazon. In Brazil in 1992 the Australian weekly magazine *People* reported that a small aeroplane had a near miss with a huge flying reptile as it was about to land. One of the 24 passengers allegedly said,

"this was a classic case of a white pterodactyl with a giant wingspan. Of course, I've heard the rumours for many years that these prehistoric creatures still roamed the Amazon. But I was sceptical like everybody else. But this wasn't an aeroplane or a UFO flying besides us. It was a pterodactyl."

Demon Flyer

The Ropen ('demon flyer') is said to live in caves on the islands of Rumbutyo, New Britain and Umboi, Papua New Guinea. It has a 1–1.2 metre wingspan, a long beak and a long tail with a diamond–shaped end. The Ropen flies at night and has a nasty habit of attacking funerals because it likes to eat rotting human flesh. An even bigger beast can be found on mainland Papua New Guinea. It is called the Duah and has a 6 metre wingspan, a long neck and a *Pteranodon*–like bony head crest.

Mistaken Identity?

* With a monstrous 7.5 metre wingspan the condor-like giant teratorn, *Argentavis magnificens* was the largest bird to ever to fly. With a wingspan of 3.7 metres the wandering albatross has the largest wingspan of any living bird (larger than many large pterosaurs). Unfortunately it lives in the remote Southern Ocean around Antarctica!
* If you are in the right part of the world you may be able to see the massive Andean condor and the incredible Eurasian black vulture. Both have wingspans of about 3 metres.
* A number of birds with long necks and bills could easily be mistaken for extinct pterosaurs. Compare, for example, pictures of herons, cranes, pelicans, swans, ibis and storks in flight to pictures of pterosaurs.
* In flight, large fruit bats like the Bismarck flying fox of Indonesia and Papua New Guinea look very prehistoric.
* If in Africa take special care not to confuse pterosaurs with prehistoric–looking shoebills (*Balaeniceps rex*). Also look out for hammer headed fruit bats, they have wingspans of around 1 metre and the male has a monstrous horse–like head. Although it lives in Africa, monster hunters have noted that hammer headed fruit bats match descriptions of the Jersey Devil – a bat winged, horse–headed demon said to inhabit the Jersey Pine Barrens in the United States.

See *How to Spot Batman* for more about hammer headed fruit bats.

How to Deal with Killer Crocodiles

They're big, bad and you're definitely on the menu. Read this if you want to survive.

* Crocodilians (crocodiles and their relatives) are old. Crocodile–like animals first appeared about the same time as dinosaurs 251–200 million years ago. Dinosaurs and crocodilians (along with pterosaurs) shared the same early ancestors – the archosaurs ('ruling reptiles').

* Dinosaurs had their chance, but crocodiles came out on top. Twenty-three crocodilian species survive to the present day. No one is sure why crocodilians outlasted the dinosaurs, but being super–tough, adaptable and clever certainly helped.

Crocodile V Dinosaur

* Some of the largest crocodilians that ever lived would have EATEN some fairly large dinosaurs. A Cretaceous croc called *Sarcosuchus imperator* ('flesh crocodile emperor') lived in Africa. It grew to enormous sizes (12 metres long weighing 8 tonnes – as heavy as some of the heaviest carnivorous dinosaurs, including *Tyrannosuarus rex*). Dino–chomping *Deinosuchus hatcheri* (meaning 'terrible crocodile') lived in the United States in the late Createaceous period, 80–73 million years ago. It was an ancient relative of alligators and may have grown up to 12 metres.

* Although larger, both *Sarcosuchus* and *Deinosuchus* looked like today's crocodiles and alligators. The design was a good one.

* It is thought that crocodiles continue to grow all their lives, and crocodiles can live for over 70 years.

* The saltwater or estuarine crocodile is thought to be the largest species alive today. On rare occasions it grows longer than 6 metres. Claims of crocodiles of 9 metres or

more are almost certainly exaggerated, but not impossible. That said, 6 metre long crocodiles weighing over a tonne are still big!

* Other crocodilians that grow up to 6 metres include the Nile crocodile of Africa, the Orinoco crocodile, The American crocodile, The American alligator and the Indian gharial.

Nile crocodile

Man–eaters

The Nile crocodile of Africa is the world's most deadly crocodilian, responsible for hundreds of deaths every year.

One legendary mega–croc is still at large in the Ruzizi River and Lake Tanganyika, Burundi (Central Africa). 'Gustave' is thought to be 6 metres long and responsible for 300 deaths.

Catching killer crocodiles

To catch a giant crocodile, construct a huge baited cage trap with floats (so the animal doesn't drown). Either tether it to the bank or secure it half in the water . Top Tip: Crocodiles prefer fresh meat to rotting meat and have a fondness for monkeys.

Warning signs

* Crocodiles are notorious man–eaters, ambush predators that usually attack people wading in the shallows (a 6 metre crocodile can lie unseen in less than a foot of water). Stay at least 3 metres from the water's edge.

* A crocodile may be seen submerging before a strike and small air bubbles could indicate the presence of a crocodile rising to the surface. However, if you are close enough to see such bubbles it is probably too late to avoid the crocs super–fast ambush.

* Crocodiles have one of the most powerful bites of any animal on earth (experts estimated the power of a *Tyrannosaurus rex* bite based on how crocodilian jaws work). Once closed however, it is quite easy to hold them closed (You may have seen experts 'wrestling' crocodiles – jumping on their backs and holding their jaws closed). Of course, no single human would be able to wrestle a 6 metre long 1–tonne Nile crocodile. They wouldn't stand a chance!

Attack!

* If you're attacked and dragged into the water, it's unlikely you'll be able to break free of the hugely powerful jaws. Your only real hope is to stab the crocodile in the eyes with a knife, a sharp object or your fingers before it drags you under, drowns then eats you.

* Crocodiles can run on land at 12–14 kph for short distances but are built for explosive surprise attacks as opposed to chasing down prey. In the unlikely event of being chased run as fast as you can in a straight line (away from the crocodile, preferably). It will tire after 30 metres and then you'll be fine.

Saltwater crocodile

How to Solve Lake Monsters Mysteries

Whether you want to solve the mystery of Loch Ness or find out why the ducks are disappearing in your local pond, the following guide will help.

Lake monster

Top 10 Lake Monster Mysteries

1. Nessie. Loch Ness in the Scottish Highlands is 36 km long and 230 metres deep in places. Over the years, there have been more than 3000 documented sightings of the most famous, hunted and photographed monsters on the planet as well as many thousands of unrecorded sightings. Some of the most interesting sightings (particularly for trackers) are those that have taken place on land:

* In the late 1800s a grey long necked beast was seen on several occasions waddling into Loch Ness from nearby woodland.
* On a sunny day in July 1933, a large, long necked creature slithered across the road in front of a car driven by a Mr and Mrs Spicer, then disappeared into the loch. The couple found traces of disturbance in the bracken where the monster had emerged. Mr Spicer said the creature was "the nearest approach to a dragon or a prehistoric animal I have ever seen in my life".
* A similar sighting took place on a moonlit night in January 1934 when Arthur Grant claimed he nearly crashed into the monster on his motorcycle!

RANGER TIP Beware of tricksters. In 1933 The Daily Mail Newspaper sponsored African big game hunter Marmaduke Wetherell to track down the monster. He soon found tracks belonging to a huge beast and had plaster casts made. Was the mystery about to be solved? No. After analysis by the Natural History Museum in London it was revealed the tracks were from a hippo–foot umbrella stand!

2. **'Mokele-mbembe'**. Could dinosaurs be living in the remote jungles of Africa? Some people believe they do. Most of the action centres on Lake Tele, a large but shallow lake surrounded by swamps, deep in the Congo Jungle. Local pygmies have named an elephant sized, long–necked beast Mokèlé–mbèmbé (one who stops the flow of rivers). On a 1932 expedition to nearby Cameroon legendary monster hunter Ivan T. Sanderson thought he saw a Mokèlé–mbèmbé and found 'vast hippo–like tracks'. He believed they came from a sauropod dinosaur. There have been many other sightings. During a 1983 expedition to Lake Tele Zoologist Dr Marcellin Agnagna of Brazzaville Zoo saw a reptilian creature raise its head its head and neck out of the water close to the shore. See *How to Track Dinosaurs* if you plan to launch your own Mokèlé–mbèmbé expedition.

3. **Lliamna Lake Monsters**. Lliamna Lake in remote south–western Alaska might well contain monsters. The lake is huge – 130 km long and 40 km wide covering an area of 3000 square kilometres. The maximum depth of the lake is 301 metres. Native Indians were once fearful of 'giant blackfish' that were capable of biting holes through canoes. Then, in the 1940's intrepid bush pilots flying over the lake began reporting strange slender–bodies of sturgeon–like fish ranging from 3–9 metres in length. Sightings continue, but the mystery remains.

4. **Tianchi Lake Monster.** 373 metre deep Tianchi Lake (Heaven Lake) lies within the cone of a volcano at an altitude of 2198 metres in the Changbai Mountains, China. A high–ranking government official reported seeing the seal–like head of a 9 metre long monster in 1968. Since then scores of tourists and serious researchers have watched, photographed and filmed individuals and groups of creatures 'playing' in the lake.

5. **Nahuelito**. Also known as the Patagonian plesiosaur, 'Nahuelito' is supposed to live in Nahuel Huapi Lake in Argentina.

Part of a national park, the lake covers an area of 544 square kilometres at an altitude 767 metres in the Andean foothills. The lake is super–deep – over 425 metres. Early reports of crushed bushes and huge tracks leading to the lake as well as many recent sightings make Nahuelito an exciting monster to study.

6. Champ. Lake Champlain is huge – 172 km long and up to 23 km wide. It occupies parts of the US states of New York and Vermont, and Quebec in Canada. Unlike Storsie, 'Champ' is protected in law 'from any wilful act resulting in death, injury or harassment.' Champ is a real 'show off', making regular appearances alongside boats and 'posing' for photos.

7. Ogopogo. Canada has more lake monsters than any other country on earth. 'Ogopogo' is the name given to the horse–headed serpent of 130 km long Lake Okanagan, British Columbia, Canada. This famous lake monster should be easy to find. Native Indians thought the evil beast's lair was in a cave under a place called Rattlesnake Island.

8. Morag. Reaching depths of 310 metres Loch Morar in the Scottish Highlands is the deepest freshwater lake in the British Isles. 'Morag' is a 6–9 metre long serpent–like beast seen by many people over hundreds of years. Duncan McDonnell and William Simpson claim to have struck a 9 metre long brown 'eel' with their boat one evening in August 1969. Terrified (neither man could swim), McDonnell hit the beast with an oar (which snapped) and Simpson shot at it with his .22 rifle. The monster dived out of sight.

9. Selma. Looking like a giant horse–headed eel, the black–eyed monster of the beautiful Lake Seljordsvatnet near Seljord, Norway has been frightening people since 1750. 'Selma' has been the focus of a great deal of recent research (including attempts to catch a baby monster in a giant eel trap). The 3–12 metre long beast is apparently sometimes seen slithering along the shore.

10. Storsie. There have been more than 200 sightings of Storsie, a Nessie–like monster in 74 m deep, 464 square kilometre Storsjön (The Great Lake), in Western Sweden. Storsie was a protected species until a local man was refused an application to search for the beast's eggs (he wanted to hatch some baby monsters!) The law was changed, as it was decided an undiscovered animal couldn't possibly be protected.

Top Theories

Here are the top lake monster theories:

Giant eels. If European and American eels grew to be 6 metres long it would solve many a lake monster mystery. Unfortunately, they don't – or at least there is no evidence that they do. Capturing a record–breaking eel in Loch Ness or any other freshwater lake would be amazing since eels more than 1 metre long are considered extremely large. Conger and moray eels are much bigger beasts but are found in saltwater.

Catfish

Monster catfish. 'Giant eels' are more likely to be large (possibly out–of–place) catfish. The wels catfish (*Silurus glanis*), for example, is native to central Europe and western Asia but can be found in ponds, lakes and rivers in Britain. They may grow to be 4.5 metres long. For more about catfish see *How to Fish For Monsters*.

Super sturgeon. Prehistoric–looking giant sturgeons have bony plates and may be mistaken for crocodiles and alligators. They are likely lake monsters in North American lakes and could occasionally visit European lakes like Loch Ness. Most Sturgeon live in the sea, and like salmon, travel up rivers once in a while to spawn. The beluga sturgeon of southern Russia is the biggest – growing up to 7.5 metres. Other 'monstrous' fish include the 3 metre alligator gar of North and Central America and pike species which may grow to up to 1.8 metres long.

Prehistoric beast. Could a few prehistoric beasts continue to exist in places like Loch Ness? Just a few? The problem is it would take more than a few. For any species to breed successfully many individuals are needed. Nessie should be a common sight! Another problem for plesiosaur / dinosaur fans is that most of the lakes (other than Lake Tele) are cold – the last place you would expect to find reptiles. And even if prehistoric beasts do live in lakes, why haven't any bodies turned up?

Mistaken identity. Mirages, monster–shaped driftwood, the wake (waves) from boats, long necked birds, swimming deer and otters travelling in a line (ducking and diving to make 'humps') have fooled many people. Some deep lakes like Loch Ness have underwater waves (known as a seiche). They can sweep up debris and bring it to the surface.

Moray eel

Are lake monsters dragons?

Dracontology is the study of dragons. People who study lake monsters use the same word to describe their work, but it doesn't mean that they believe that lake monsters are dragons. Whether lake monsters are the same as the dragons of old is, however, still an interesting question. According to legend, a 'dragon' can be heard to roar on stormy nights in little Lough Brin, County Kerry, Ireland. Monsters have been spotted in the lough fairly recently, including a 3 metre black animal that looked half seal, half dragon. Makes you wonder, doesn't it?

Expedition Tips

* Do some background research. What does the monster look like? Where and when is the monster usually seen? What was the weather like? Talk to witnesses about their sightings, if possible.
* Make a list of local wildlife. Otter, swimming deer and long necked birds can appear monster–like. Local anglers will be able to tell you about the sorts of fish to be found in the lake and might know about local legends.
* Don't forget your camera! Make a photographic record of your expedition and remember – a good lake monster photo could be worth a fortune!
* 'Read' the water. Evidence suggests Morag and Nessie are most likely to be seen in shallow bays near river and stream mouths, perhaps because this is where most fish are found. 'Drop offs' (where shallow water suddenly becomes deeper are also good places to find fish. Polarised sunglasses will help you see into the water.
* Search the shore. Look for tracks and tell–tale marks (see *How to Track Monsters* and *How to Track Dinosaurs*) teeth, bones and bodies.
* Watch and listen. Use stalking techniques to monitor the lake. Camouflage yourself or build a hide and use

binoculars or telescopes if you have them. Listen quietly for strange sounds like splashes, watch for large swirling eddies and jumping fish.

* You could try 'baiting' the beast to the surface (if permitted). Use bread, sweet corn or dog biscuits to attract smaller fish that will attract predators. Fill an old sock with meaty/fishy bait, tie it to a float such as a plastic milk carton then secure to an anchor on the bank to tempt giant catfish and eels to the surface. Another type of 'bait' is light (especially green light). Light attracts little creatures, which then attract bigger creatures. A traditional method of night fishing requires lanterns to be held over the sides of boats to attract fish.

* Search for eyeshine. Crocodiles, alligators and caymans can be spotted at night by their red eyeshine. Reptilian lake monsters might also have red eyeshine.

* Certain predatory fish (e.g. North American walleye) can also be spotted by their eyeshine. (See H*ow to Spot Monster Eyeshine*).

* Study maps. Could the beast be travelling overland at night to nearby ponds and lakes? Look for features on maps like woodland next to the lake that could be used as monster hideouts.

* Go techno. The techniques in this book should be more than enough to uncover the identity of a beast, but if you've got pots of cash camera traps on the bank, research boats, diving equipment, sonar fish finders, night vision cameras, thermal imaging cameras, hydrophones (to listen to underwater sounds) and underwater cameras might help. On the hand, they might not. Lake monsters don't like being 'studied'. Most sightings happen when people are least expecting them.

* Catch the beast! As a last resort, you might have to catch the beast. You'll need permission to set a trap and the correct permits to fish. See *How to Trap Lake Monsters* and *How to Fish for Monsters.*

How to Trap Lake Monsters

One of most irresponsible attempts to catch a lake monster involved the use of explosives. It nearly worked. In 1954 Georgina Carberry and three companions were fishing on Lough Fadda, Ireland. Whilst taking a tea break the group were frightened by a huge creature with a gaping mouth, a slithering coiled body and a dragon–like forked tail. Terrified, they fled. Men were sent to the lough with guns but the monster didn't reappear.

The Loch Ness Investigation Bureau sent an expedition team over to Ireland to catch the beast, led by Captain Lionel Leslie. In 1965 Leslie set off five pounds of gelignite at the same place Georgina and her companions had their encounter. Seconds after the explosion, a large black object broke the surface and thrashed about. Everyone present agreed there was a monster in Lough Fadda.

Monster traps

Giant eel traps are a more sensible approach to monster catching. Eel traps have been used in attempts to catch Nessie and Selma (the monster of Lake Seljordsvatnet in Norway). Although they failed, giant eel traps should work if we assume lake monsters are carnivores (meat eaters). Herbivores (plant eaters) would have to be caught by trawling the lake with a large fishing net with floats at the top and weights at the bottom called a seine – or captured on land.

Eel traps have been used for centuries and were traditionally made like wicker baskets. They can be made from wire mesh, netting, converted lobster pots or fabric. The basic idea is that the eel (or catfish) is attracted to a pouch filled with bait (offal, herring etc.) through a cone–shaped entrance or a fabric 'tunnel'. Once inside it finds it difficult to find the entrance again. Most eel traps work on exactly the same principle as the bottle trap.

How to Make a Bottle Trap

Making a bottle trap is good training for the day you construct a giant monster trap. Larger (5 litre) plastic bottles baited with meat will also catch eels.:

You will need:

* **2 plastic bottles (2–5 litres)**
* **Sharp scissors**
* **An average–size nail for making holes in the bottles**
* **Pliers**
* **String**
* **A source of heat such as a stove or candle**
* **A bowl of cold water**
* **An adult helper**

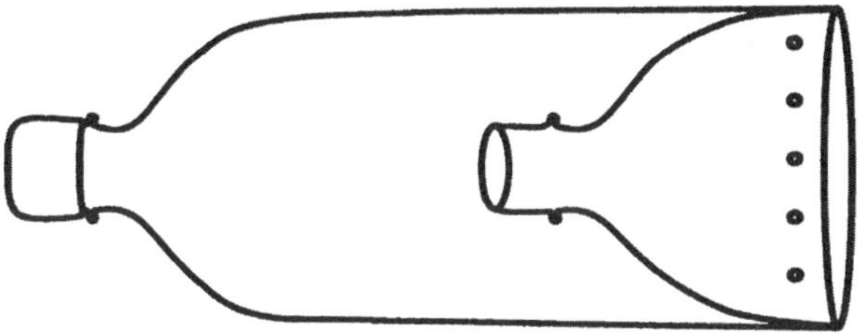

1. Take one of the bottles and cut off the bottom third (leave the screw cap on)

2. Take the other bottle and cut the top off below where the sloping neck straightens out. Take the top screw cap off.

3. For the following stages you'll need your adult helper. Make sure you are near your stove or burning candle with the bowl of water to hand. Fit the smaller funnel inside the larger funnel.

4. Get your adult helper to heat the nail up whilst holding it in the pliers. Make even–spaced holes where the two bottles overlap (10 or so should be enough). Cool the nail in the bowl of water. Loop the string in and out of the holes to hold the two pieces together and tie a knot. Reheat the nail and make holes in the trap so that the trap sinks when it is placed in water.

5. Put some bread (or meat) in the bottle as bait, tie the trap to an anchor and sink it in a shallow stream or pond overnight. Check daily to see what you've caught.

How to Avoid the Jaws of Giants

You are leading an expedition to discover new species of plants and animals in an unexplored part of Africa. The only way to get there is by canoe, along a hippo–infested river. You need to give your team some practical safety advice. Here's what you should tell them.

Hippo Danger

* One of Africa's most dangerous animals, male hippos stand 1.5 metres tall and weigh 3.2 tonnes. Mostly herbivores (they sometimes scavenge meat but it is rare), hippos have dagger–like lower canine teeth more than 30 cm long. Their powerful jaws are capable of biting a crocodile (or human) in half.
* Hippos sometimes attack boats. Bang the sides of your canoe with your paddle to let them know you are there.
* When angry, hippos will open their mouths displaying their teeth before making short warning charges through the water. This means 'back off!'
* The less water, the more stressed hippos feel. As you approach hippos will head for deeper water, so stick to the shallows and try not to block a hippo's path back to deeper water.
* Keep well away from lone bulls and above all, keep away from females with young.
* Game rangers are taught never to get between a hippo and the water. This is because when a grazing hippo is disturbed it will almost certainly panic and attack (hippos venture onto land to graze at night). If a hippo charges you on land, don't hang around – run for your life!
* You can avoid surprising hippos on dry land by looking out for their worn paths and keeping away from thick bushes near water. Never camp in hippo habitat.

RANGER TIP: Look out for bubbles and V–shaped waves hurtling toward your canoe. You are under attack, it is time to get to safety (if you can). As a last resort, slap your paddle hard against the water. With luck the noise will be scare the hippo off.

How to Spot Sea–monsters

The seaside is a great place to hunt for monsters. After all, 71% of planet earth is ocean and it is full of enormous, amazing and unusual creatures.

Sightings of sea monsters go back a long way. Here is an account from 1555 about a 60 metre long, 6 metre wide sea serpent that lived in caves near Bergen, Norway:

'On bright summer nights this serpent leaves the caves to eat calves, lambs and pigs, or it fares out to the sea and feeds on sea nettles, crabs and similar marine animals. It has ell-long hair hanging from its neck, sharp black scales and flaming red eyes. It attacks vessels, grabs and swallows people, as it lifts itself up like a column from the water.'

* ell = an old unit of measurement, from the elbow to the wrist or fingertips

And a more recent account, from Filey, Yorkshire (UK). The story was reported in the Daily Telegraph in 1934. One night local coastguard Mr Wilkinson Herbert was walking along Filey Brig, a spur of rocks running into the sea when;

'Suddenly I heard a growling like a dozen dogs ahead, walking nearer I switched on my torch and was confronted by a huge neck, six yards in front of me, rearing up 8 ft. high! The head was a startling sight– huge eyes like saucers, glaring at me, the creature's mouth was a foot wide and neck would be a yard around. The monster appeared as startled as I was. Shining my torch along the ground I saw a body about 30 ft. long. I thought this was no place for me and from a distance I threw stones at the creature. It moved away growling fiercely and I saw the huge black body had two humps on it and four short legs with huge flappers on them. I could not see any tail. It moved quickly, rolling from side to side, and went into the sea. From the cliff top I looked down and saw two eyes like torchlight's shining out to sea 300 yards away. It was a most gruesome and thrilling experience. I have seen big animals abroad, but nothing like this.'

In 1965 Belgian cryptozoologist Dr Bernard Heuvalmans looked at hundreds of sea monster reports like the report you have just read and put them into categories. Here are his main types:

* Long–necked – 4.6 to 18 metre sea lion– like creature with four flippers and a long neck.
* Many–humped – 18 to 30 metre creature with lots of humps – possibly an ancient whale.
* Merhorse – 17 to 30 metre creature with a long neck, large eyes and a horse–like mane.
* Many–finned – 18 to 21 metre armoured creature with lots of fins.
* Super otter – 20 to 30 metres long – like a very large otter.
* Marine saurian – 15 to 18 metre crocodile–like sea monsters. One was reported in 1915 by a German submarine, U–28 Schmidt. After firing a torpedo at a British ship in the North Atlantic, the crew saw an 18 metre long crocodile–like creature shoot out of the water.
* Super eel – 9 to 30 metres long – the classic sea serpent. In 1848 the crew of a British ship, HMS Daedalus saw an 18 metre long, 40 cm thick 'snake' off the coast of Namibia, Africa. In 1875 the entire crew of the cargo ship Pauline saw a 50 metre long, 2–2.5 metre wide sea serpent crush a sperm whale in its coils off the northeast coast of Brazil.

Prehistoric sea monsters

* Plesiosaurs were aquatic reptiles with flippers that breathed air (they were not dinosaurs, although they lived at the same time). There were two groups: 'true' plesiosaurs with long serpent–like necks and small heads and pliosaurs with big heads, strong jaws and short necks. Fossil remains of one of the most fearsome creatures of all time, a pliosaur code–named 'Predator X' was found on the island of Svalbard near the North Pole in 2008. It had a head twice the size of a *Tyrannosaurus rex*, was 15 metres long and would have weighed 45 tonnes.

* When the plesiosaurs declined towards the end of the Cretaceous period (144–65 million years ago), the fearsome mososaurs took over the oceans. Whereas plesiosaurs used their flippers to propel themselves and steered with their tail, mososaurs used their tails to propel themselves and used their flippers to steer. Relatives of monitor lizards and snakes, giant mososaurs like *Tylosaurus* and *Hainosaurus* also grew to be 15 metres in length.

Deep ocean facts

The deepest part of the oceans is the 2542 km long Mariana Trench in the Pacific Ocean between Japan and Papua New Guinea.

The deepest part of the trench is called Challenger Deep. It is the lowest point on earth; reaching a depth of about 11,000 metres. Since Mount Everest reaches an altitude of 'only' 8848 metres, the summit would still be 2000 metres below the surface if the mountain was placed within it. Still can't picture it? If you ever travel by aeroplane, take a look out of the window in the middle of your journey and imagine you're on a boat. 11,000 metres is a typical passenger airline cruising altitude.

There are three main 'zones of life' in the ocean. Life is found at all depths but decreases the deeper you go. The first zone is the shallowest, extending from the surface to about 200 metres and is called the epipelagic meaning 'upon the sea'. The epipelagic is lit by sunlight. The next zone, called the mesopelagic meaning 'middle sea' is sometimes called 'the twilight zone' because the upper part gets sunlight during the day but the deeper parts at about 1000 metres are permanently dark. The lowest zone is forever dark – the abyss.

Sea monsters today

* Found mostly in warm and tropical seas (except the Mediterranean), the harmless filter feeding whale shark is the largest fish on earth and can grow up to 18 metres long and weigh 20 tonnes. It can be seen in the spring and summer when it feeds at the surface. The 11 metre long basking shark is the second–largest fish and is widespread in temperate waters. They are sometimes seen off the British coast and sightings seem to correspond to sea monster 'hotspots' around Cornwall and West Wales (See *Top Destinations*). Another huge filter feeding shark, the 5–metre megamouth was only discovered in 1976!

* Great White Sharks are 6 metre long killing machines. You are most likely to be attacked in America, (especially the West Coast), Australia and South Africa. If attacked, fight back. Attack the shark's sensitive nose, eyes and gills. Get out of the water as quickly as possible.

* **RANGER TIP**: Bull sharks are even more dangerous than great white sharks. They are extremely aggressive and likely to come close to shore.

* If you thought great white sharks were scary, you haven't heard of their extinct relative megalodon. With a bite more powerful than *Tyrannosauros rex*, megalodon grew 15 metres long and was one of the largest carnivorous fish to ever exist.

* Some sharks are weird. Frilled sharks have changed little since prehistoric times and are considered to be 'living fossils'. They look like large eels with massive heads and could easily be mistaken for sea serpents.

* Squid can be scary. Humboldt squid or diablos rojos (red devils) are cannibals and love nothing more than attacking and eating weaker members of their own species. They can be aggressive and are certainly dangerous, quite capable latching on to careless divers, dragging them down into the dark depths and tearing them to pieces with their razor–sharp beaks (which are a bit like parrots beaks). They live in the Sea of Cortez off the coast of California and Mexico and grow up to 2.5 metres long.

* Monster squid – the Kraken of legend, definitely exist. Giant squid live in deep oceans throughout the world and can grow up to 13 metres long. The colossal squid of the Southern Ocean is even bigger and is known to grow up to 14 metres long (both the giant squid and the colossal squid may grow larger but this can't be proved).

* Growing up to 18 metres long and weighing up to 50 tonnes, sperm whales can be found in all the world's oceans except the arctic and are thought to be the biggest predators on the planet. They eat giant squid and colossal squid, and often have large circular scars from suckers – the result of deep–sea battles between monsters of the deep. The tough beaks of monster squid aren't digested and remain in the whale's stomach. Since marine biologists can measure them and estimate the size of squid's body, the evidence suggests huge squids larger than any seen or caught exist.

* Weighing up to 180 tonnes and growing up to 30 metres long, blue whales are thought to be the largest animal to exist on Earth – bigger than the biggest dinosaurs.

* With flippers, streamlined bodies and fearsome teeth, seals can resemble extinct plesiosaurs. Leopard seals and southern elephant seals grow to enormous sizes. Southern elephant seals are the largest of all. These powerful predators live in the Antarctic and sub Antarctic and can grow up to 6.5 metres long and weigh 3.5 tonnes.

* Shimmering deep-sea dwelling oarfish are real-life sea serpents in every way (except that they are harmless). They grow up to 11 metres long and are rarely seen. You are most likely to see one that has died or is dying and washes up on a beach.

* Shipwreck–loving conger eels grows large enough to be described as sea serpents. Conger eels can grow over 2 metres long and have sharp teeth and powerful jaws. In 2004 a scuba diver claimed he was attacked and nearly dragged away by a 3.6 metre European conger whilst diving a shipwreck in the North Sea off St Andrews, Scotland.

Top destinations

If you want to see a sea monster, try the following top destinations:

Cadboro Bay (Canada). Sandy beaches, secret coves and a famous sea-serpent make Cadboro Bay in Victoria, British Columbia a fantastic sea-monster spotting destination. There have been hundreds of sightings of *Cadborosaurus* or 'Caddy' along the Pacific Northwest coast of North America. Witnesses describe a Nessie-like monster – a huge serpent with humps, a long neck and a horse-like head.

Chesapeake Bay (US). The site of an ancient meteorite impact, Chesapeake Bay is the largest estuary in North America, stretching from southern Virginia to northern Maryland. This popular destination has beaches, abundant wildlife, fishing, boating and sailing. It also has a famous monster, known as 'Chessie'. Huge numbers of people have reported seeing the monster, described as 9–12 metres long with a dark snakelike body like that of an anaconda. Sea monster spotters should be aware that the bay is also home to huge prehistoric–looking Atlantic sturgeon (a species known to leap out of water) and is visited by the occasional manatee (large, plant eating marine mammals believed to have evolved from an animal related to elephants).

Falmouth Bay (UK). Lovely coastal towns, sandy beaches and beautiful countryside make Falmouth Bay, Cornwall a top seaside destination. Sightings of the plesiosaur-like Morgawr go back to at least 1906. Hotspots include Pendennis Point, Rosemullion Head near Mawnan and nearby Gerran's Bay (fisherman are said to have accidentally caught a sea serpent in their nets here in 1876). It is possible that Morgawr occasionally travels north to visit the coast of West Wales – another sea monster hotspot (be aware that whales and basking sharks visit the coasts of Cornwall and West Wales). While if you're in the Falmouth Bay area you should pay a visit to Owlman's haunt in nearby Mawnan (See *How to See Monster Eyeshine*), as well as Dartmoor and Bodmin Moor — famous haunts of mystery big cats.

Beachcombing for globsters

* On the beach keep an eye out for fossils, dinosaur tracks and 'globsters'. Globsters are huge lumps of rotting flesh that might be the remains of sea monsters.

* A globster washed up on the shores of Stronsa Island, Scotland (one of the Orkney Islands) on September 26th 1808. The 17 metres long serpent–like remains appeared to have a 4.6 metre 'neck', a hairy 'mane' and three sets of 'legs' (more likely to have been fins).

* Another weird creature washed up on the shore of Margate Beach in Kwa–Zulu Natal, South Africa on November 1st, 1922. The previous evening several people claimed they watched a titanic sea– battle worthy of the movie Godzilla between three huge sea monsters!

RANGER TIP: When a basking shark dies it is known to rot in such a way that after a while it looks uncannily like a plesiosaur. Unusual beaked whales (which have huge heads with duck–like beaks) have also fooled a few people.

How to Paddle a Kayak

Kayaks are perfect for spotting or escaping from swamp beasts, lake monsters and sea serpents. Here are some tips to get you started.

WARNING: Kayaking is a dangerous activity. This beginner's guide is in no way meant to take the place of a formal course run by a certified instructor. Make sure you have the correct safety equipment, including a lifejacket.

The top of a kayak is the deck, the bottom is the hull, the front is the bow and the back is the stern.

There are many types of kayak but you will probably learn with a wide, flat–bottomed recreational or 'rec' kayak designed for use on calm water. Sit–inside models have a cockpit and you can attach a spray deck (a cover to stop water getting in). Sit–on–top kayaks are safe, fun, easy to use and popular with anglers – but you are more likely to get wet! There are a range of various hard–bodied kayaks and inflatable kayaks. Besides being light and portable (useful for expeditions), inflatable kayaks are very easy to master.

Specialised kayaks include long and narrow sea kayaks for use on large choppy lakes and open sea and whitewater kayaks for fast flowing rivers.

Getting in

Use your paddle for support at awkward launch sites. Place your paddle at 90 degrees on the boat just behind the cockpit with one blade flat on the shore. Hold the shaft behind your back, squat low beside the kayak and gripping both the shaft and the cockpit in one hand, ease yourself in.

Holding the paddle

Kayak paddles have two blades on the ends of a shaft. Some blades don't have a top or bottom (they look the same either way up). Others are tapered (sloping) and get narrower towards the bottom. One trick to tell you are holding a tapered paddle the right way up is to look for a label. If the writing is the right way up, so are the paddles.

Blades often have a slight cupped shape that catches the water (called the power face). It's like the shape of your hand when swimming. When you swim you pull yourself through the water with the palm side of your hand, not the back. It's the same with the blades of a paddle: the power face should face you when you paddle.

Beginners may find it easier if both blades are fixed to the shaft in a straight line – 'unfeathered' (see below). However, if you have feathered (offset) blades you will need to decide which hand will control the paddle. If you are right handed, that hand usually holds the shaft. If you are left–handed the left hand usually controls the paddle.

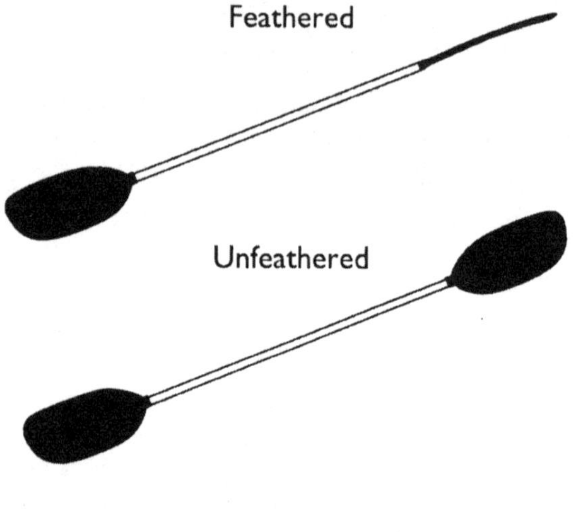

With knuckles lined–up to the top edge of the blade, the controlling hand stays in the same position at all times. The grip with the other hand is loosened between each paddle stroke so that you can rotate the shaft with your control hand.

RANGER TIP Find the correct hand position by placing the centre of the paddle shaft on top of your head and holding it so your elbows from right angles:

Get paddling

There's a swamp beast on your tail. Time to get paddling!

1. Sit comfortably upright with your knees slightly bent.

2. You need to dip one of the blades fully into the water near your toes. Don't lean forward to do this. Holding your paddle with a relaxed but firm grip, reach forward by twisting your upper body and push your shoulder forward while reaching out with your arm.

3. Once the blade is fully in the water pull on the paddle close alongside the boat to drive it forward. Use your upper body to power the stroke, instead of just relying on your arms. Keep your other hand at about shoulder level.

4. When the paddle reaches your hip, lift the blade out of the water and repeat steps 1–3 on the opposite side.

5. To turn repeat steps 1–4 but keep your hands low and sweep the blade as far out to the side as possible on the opposite side of the boat to the direction you want to turn.

How to Fish For Monsters

If you're new to fishing, visit your local tackle shop. In most cases the owner will be happy to answer sensible questions about fishing licences, equipment for beginners, free fishing grounds, fees, techniques, local clubs, training, and even local legends about 'the one that got away.'

An all-round telescopic rod starter kit complete with reel, floats, weights, lures and selection of hooks is a good option for the beginner. Telescopic rods are portable and you may be travelling on foot to remote locations. They are great for camping trips and moving quickly from spot to spot. Beginner's kits sometimes come with handy instruction booklets to get you started.

Monster fish

Fishing for freshwater 'monsters' (big predators) involves two main methods: bait fishing and lure fishing:

Note: The true sportsman always returns 'monsters' unharmed back into the water.

Bait fishing is a good all-round method. It involves using bait such as a maggot, worms, fish or luncheon meat suspended beneath a float on one or more hooks or weights keeping the bait at the bottom (known as ledgering).

Lure fishing is used specifically to catch fish that like to eat other fish (pike family etc.). Some lures look like prey species and some lures – called 'spoons' flash and vibrate mimicking a small fish. The lure is cast into the water and reeled in so that to a big predator it appears to be swimming through the water.

Freshwater eels

Both the European freshwater eel *Anguilla anguilla* and the American eel *Anguilla rostrata* spawn in the Sargasso Sea between Bermuda and Puerto Rico. Ocean currents carry the tiny larval eels past the coast of North America, but only the American Eels stay. European eels take three years to reach Europe. They enter rivers and begin new nocturnal lives in freshwater. Mature 'silver' eels begin their epic quest to return to the Sargasso Sea after feeding and growing for 6-20 years.

Exceptional freshwater eels can grow up to 1.3 metres long. They are found in the most unlikely ponds and streams, helped by the fact they can absorb oxygen through their skin and travel over land.

Some people claim famous lake monsters are stranded mutant giant eels. Windermere in the English Lake District is supposed to be home to a 6 metre long eel. In 2006 'it' (whatever it was) hit the headlines when it frightened a university teacher and his wife.

Main fishing methods: Bait fishing (night)

How to sniggle for eels

Eels are usually active at night but they can be 'sniggled' from their daytime hideouts, photographed and released. Here's how:

A large barbless fishing hook
A metre or so of strong line
A short stick broken at one end
Towel or unhooking mat
Forceps to remove the hook
Some worms

1. Find an area of still or slow-running shallow water no deeper than your knees where you suspect large eels may be lurking.

2. Tie the line to the hook and thread on the worm leaving the point of the hook free.

3. Fix the end of the hook loosely into the broken end of the stick where it is soft and may be pulled out easily.

4. Hold the line in one hand, and the stick in the other and wade into the water looking for eel hideouts (holes in the bank, under rocks and in crevices).

5. Poke the end of the stick with the hook and worm into holes. If an eel is there, it will usually go for the worm.

6. When an eel bites and you feel the stick is free, throw the stick to shore and give the line a sharp pull to set the hook.

7. Slowly work the eel free. If it's a big one you could be in for a fight!

Eels need to be handled with care (don't squeeze them tightly) and with wet hands since the protective layer of slime can easily be damaged. Note: Whatever your method, if an eel swallows the hook do not try to retrieve it. Cut the line as close to the lips as possible.

Catfish

The hideous wels catfish (*Silurus glanis*) is native to eastern and central Europe and western Asia but has been introduced to many other areas. Found in deep water in reedy lakes and slow-flowing rivers, these monster catfish grow to about 4.5 metres long and weigh up to 300 kg. This makes them even larger than the famous Mekong giant catfish (*Pangasianodon gigas*) of Southeast Asia.

Wels are mainly active at night and feed on almost anything – amphibians, fish, waterbirds and even the occasional small dog!

The fearsome **goonch** (*Bagarius yarelli*) is perhaps the world's scariest big catfish. It is unusual because it has extremely sharp teeth. The goonch has recently been accused of drowning and eating people in the Kali River, India.

Main fishing methods: Bait fishing

Pike

Pike are long, torpedo-like predatory fish with powerful jaws. They are found in weedy lowland lakes, large slow moving rivers and flooded gravel pits. Northern Pike (*Esox lucius*) of Europe and North America may grow up to 1.4 metres long. The North American muskellunge (*Esox masquinongy*) may grow up to 1.8 metres long.

In the summer of 1999 a water-skier on Llangorse Lake in Wales was attacked by a Northern Pike and needed hospital treatment for wounds to his foot.

Main Fishing Methods: Bait and lure fishing

Pike

Attack of the lake monster

Beware of fishing in little Loch Dubh, Ireland. Alphonsus Mullaney claimed he was fishing for pike or perch in the loch with his son in March 1962 when something big took the bate. Annoyed at being 'caught' a cow-sized creature that looked like a hippo with a white horn on its head tried to leave the loch to attack the pair.

Alligator gar (*Atractosteus spatula*).

An incredible armoured giant fish that looks like a huge pike with the head of an alligator. Alligator gar can grow to 3 metres long and are native to the southern United States. They are a truly dangerous fish, not for the faint hearted.

Main Fishing Methods: Bait and lure fishing

Giant tigerfish (*Hydrocynus goliath*).

Found in rivers within the Congo River Basin, Africa. The giant tigerfish is one of the scariest freshwater fish on the planet. The crocodile-like teeth of this monster can even be seen when its mouth is closed. Grows to be more than 1.8 metres long and weighs up to 57 kg.

Main fishing methods: Bait and lure Fishing.

RANGER TIP: If you're determined to catch 'a big one' nothing beats a practical lesson from qualified experts. Predator fishing courses are recommended for all levels of monster-angler, from beginners to the experienced. Again, ask at your local tackle shop.

How to Navigate

How To Use A Compass

You will need:

* **A baseplate compass**
* **A map of the relevant area**
* **A pencil**

Your quest will take you to the remote corners of the planet earth, from yeti–haunted mountains to snake infested jungles. A good compass is like a trusted friend, always ready to help you out of a tight spot. Here's how they work.

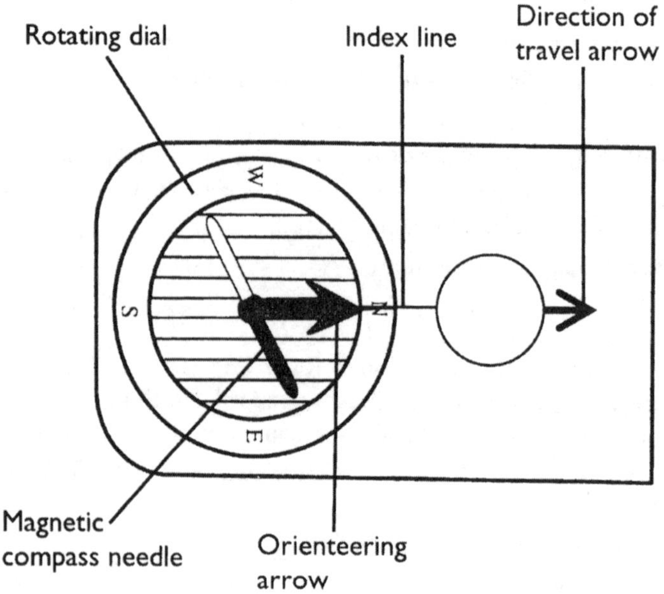

Magnetic North Pole

Planet Earth has a magnetic field, caused by the rotation of molten metals in its core.This is handy for the navigator because it means that a magnetised needle will try to align itself with this field. So when you hold a compass flat (and away from large metal objects) the red needle will always point north towards the magnetic north pole.The magnetic north pole is drifting steadily northwest over the Canadian arctic and isn't quite the same as true north, the fixed geographic North Pole. Experienced navigators adjust for this difference, called magnetic declination or magnetic deviation.

Using a compass without a map

In good visibility a baseplate compass can help you stay on the right track.

1. Look for a landmark in the distance that you want to head for (such as hill or mountain).

2. Hold the compass level at chest height (away from large metal objects) and point the direction of travel arrow where you want to go.

3. Let the red needle settle down and turn the compass housing so the orienteering arrow is over the red part of the needle.

4. If you have a pencil write and paper down the number of degrees (0–360) at the index line in case the rotating dial gets moved.

5. Experiment with your bearing, for a moment. Turn around slowly and you will see that the red compass needle and the orienteering arrow line up when compass direction of travel arrow is pointing at you destination. If you lose sight of your destination, turn around until they line up again and you'll know you're on the right track.

Get set

You can use your compass to 'set' your map of the area. When you look at a map the right way up (so you can read the words) up will be north. Now, if you hold your compass flat on a level map and rotate the map and yourself until the red compass needle points directly upwards, the map will be set. North on the map is now north on the ground. Using the map key, match the features on map to features on the ground to locate your current position and destination.

How to survive without a compass

On a clear night in the northern hemisphere you can find north by locating the North Star (Polaris). Look for the saucepan–shaped Plough, also known as the Big Dipper or Ursa Major (the Great Bear). Look for the two pointer stars that form the edge of the saucepan and draw an imaginary line between the two. Extend the imaginary line five times to arrive at the North Star.

The Plough (Big Dipper) / Polaris

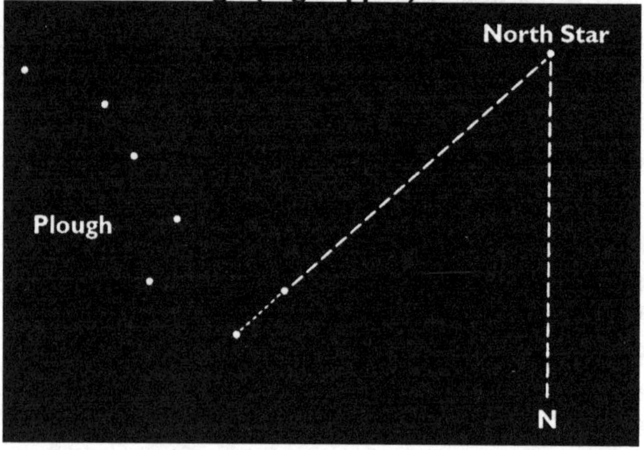

Once you've located the North Star, 'bring it down to earth'.

1. Find a long straight stick and drive it into the ground.

2. Find a shorter stick, get down low and sight across the top of it like you are aiming a gun.

3. When the star, the long stick and the short stick are in line drive the short stick into the ground. The tall stick marks north, the short stick marks south.

In the southern hemisphere you can locate south by locating the Southern Cross. Draw an imaginary line between the two stars furthest from each other. Extend the imaginary line about five times. At the end of this line draw another imaginary line towards the ground. This will point you south.

Southern Cross

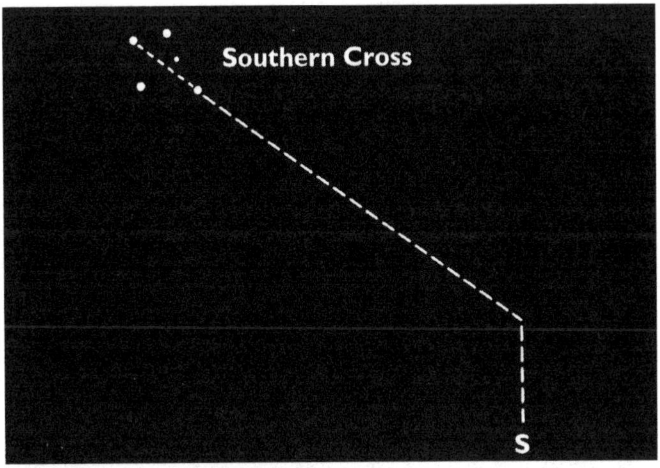

RANGER TIP: Like the sun, stars rise in the east and set in the west. If a star that is low in the sky is rising, you are facing east. If it is descending you are facing west.

Shadow Sticks

A shadow stick is a simple and effective way to find rough direction using the sun. You will need a straight stick about 1 metre long and some soft level ground free of debris.

1. Push the stick into ground and mark the tip of its shadow with a stone.

2. Wait at least 15 minutes (the longer you wait, the more accurate the reading). Mark the new position of the tip of the shadow with another stone.

3. Draw a line between the two stones. The first stone you placed is always west, the second marks east.

4. Put your left foot on the first marker and your right foot on the second marker and you will be roughly facing north.

Using a watch to navigate

* Northern Hemisphere: Hold your watch horizontal to the ground and point the hour hand at the sun. South is halfway between the hour hand and the 12 o'clock on the face.

* Southern Hemisphere: Point the 12 o'clock mark on the watch at the sun. North is halfway between the 12 o'clock mark and the hour hand.

Jungle Tips

Travelling through thick, wild animal infested jungle like the Amazon can be difficult, particularly if you don't have a map and compass. Remember these tips if you want to survive:

* If you get lost, head downhill to a river and follow it – it will lead you to civilisation.

* Don't rush – you'll get into trouble. Try to look through the trees to see the lie of the land and spot animal trails to speed up progress. Climb a tree or find high ground so that you can see the lie of the land

* When travelling through jungles and other areas with dangerous animals make lots of noise with a stick. This will give them the opportunity to get out of your way.

How to Handle Mountain Scrambles

Unless fully trained and equipped for rock climbing you should try to avoid steep ground in the mountains. It is wise however, to be prepared for unexpected obstacles and unavoidable steep ground. One mountain you may find yourself scrambling down in a hurry is Ben Mac Dui in the Scottish Highlands. It is home to a strange monster called the Big Grey Man of Ben Macdui. Some say it's a hairy Yeti–like beast – others claim it is an invisible supernatural being. Here is an account from climber John Norman Collie from 1925:

'I was returning from the cairn on the summit in a mist when I began to think I heard something else than merely the noise of my own footsteps. Every few steps I took I heard a crunch, then another crunch as if someone was walking after me but taking steps three or four times the length of my own. I said to myself "this is all nonsense". I listened and heard it again but could see nothing in the mist. As I walked on and the eerie crunch, crunch sounded behind me I was seized with terror and took to my heels, staggering blindly among the boulders for four or five miles nearly down to Rothiemurchus Forest. Whatever you make of it I do not know, but there is something very queer about the top of Ben MacDhui and I will not go back there again by myself I know.'

Scrambling Grades

Grades / classes are used to indicate how difficult and dangerous scrambling routes are in books, but do bare in mind that snow, rain and wind can make even the easiest of routes highly dangerous. Here is a summary of the UK scrambling grades and the Yosemite Decimal System, which is used in the US. Class 1 in the Yosemite Decimal System is general hiking on trails and Class 5 is rock climbing.

UK Grade 1 Yosemite Decimal System Class 2
Description
Scrambling on rough ground where you may occasionally need to use your hands.

UK Grade 2 Yosemite Decimal Class 3
Description
More difficult and potentially dangerous scrambles involving small amounts of easy rock climbing. A fall could be serious but won't always be fatal. A safety rope should be carried for emergencies.

UK Grade 3s (Serious) Yosemite Decimal Class 4
Description
A fall in this sort of terrain could well be fatal. Requires rock climbing / mountaineering experience and the use of ropes.

WARNING: Mountaineering skills like rock climbing and abseiling can only be learnt by taking a course run by a professional instructor.

Useful moves

The Boot Jam: Place your boot into a crack in the rock, using the stiff edges of the sole to support your weight. Remember that you will need to remove your foot so place your foot rather than wedging it in!

The Toe Jam: Can't get your foot into a crack? Place your toe sideways into the crack and then turn your heel in the opposite direction. As you turn your foot your toe will jam in the crack.

Edging: Make Use of the inside and outside edges of the boots to grip rough or overhanging bits of rock.

Flat Foot Friction: When walking up or down steep slabs of rock use the whole of the sole of the boot for maximum friction.

RANGER TIP: Ascending and descending steep slopes is much less tiring if you use two walking poles (or sticks). You will, however have to put them securely away if you have to scramble. You will also find steep slopes less trying if you zig zag up and down them as opposed to walking in a straight line.

Scrambling Tips

* When you have to use a combination of your hands and feet a walk becomes a scramble.
* Spend some time looking and thinking about the route ahead. Look for signs people have passed the same way.
* When climbing always maintain 3 points of contact with the rock. Only ever move one arm or one leg at a time.
* When scrambling in mountains it is essential to wear a climbing helmet. Remember also that your feet are your most important tools. You will need to wear a good hill walking or mountaineering type boot with a fairly rigid sole.
* Practice scrambling techniques on easy ground until scrambling becomes second nature.
* Remember to use you eyes: Look for solid handholds and footholds whilst maintaining an upright body position.
* If in doubt about footholds or handholds test them by giving them a gentle kick or tug.
* If you feel off–balance, stop and think. Try to stay calm and focused. Move slowly and carefully.
* Try to stay as upright as possible when climbing, letting your feet take most of the weight. They are much stronger than you arms! That said, avoid using your knees – you'll throw yourself off balance.
* When scrambling keep your arms as straight as possible and try to avoid 'hugging' the rock. This will save your strength and you are less likely to lose your balance.
* As soon as a downward climb becomes a scramble and you have to use your arms turn to face the rock.

How to Plan a Monster Hunting Expedition

An expedition is a journey with a purpose. A monster hunting expedition doesn't have to be to somewhere remote like Gobi Desert in Mongolia – it can be just as much fun to plan a monster hunting expedition to the local wood, hill or perhaps even the boating lake in a nearby park. Here's how to plan a monstrously fun adventure:

1. **Decide why** you want to launch an expedition and write down your 'expedition aim'. Look for something that really interests you. Your expedition aim might be something like:

'To investigate whether a crocodile is on the loose in the local pond'

or

'To uncover the identity of the screaming beast of Eerie Wood'.

If you're more ambitious, you might want to:

'Survey Lake Tele in the Democratic Republic of the Congo for a possible living dinosaur'.

You might also want to make a list of 'supporting objectives' – things you would also like to do if you have the time. For example, taking the ambitious Congo dinosaur expedition (above) as an example, you might also want to:

* Take photos of interesting plants and animals living in and around the lake.
* Measure the deepest point in the lake.
* Make a detailed map of the lake and the surrounding area.

2. **Choose a team**. Of course, you can undertake a solo expedition, but monster hunting can be a scary business plus it is often more fun, and safer, to go with a few like–minded friends. If you're planning a major expedition you'll need to choose people with relevant skills like knowledge of foreign languages.

3. **Write an expedition plan.** To collect all the information for your plan, you should:

* Study books, maps and previous expedition reports about the area you're travelling to (if available).
* Collect information on weather, local wildlife and possible hazards.
* Speak to local experts and park rangers. Collect as much information as possible from books, the internet and newspaper reports.

4. **Decide** on the monster hunting methods you intend to use (using this book). Remember to check with authorities like park rangers that you won't be breaking the law.

5. **Plan a route** to and from your destination then estimate how long each stage the expedition will take. Write each stage of the journey down on a 'route card' with estimated times of departure and arrival at each stage. Give this to someone responsible so if you get lost in the wilderness they will a) know roughly where you are and b) will know when to get help to you because you haven't returned.

Remember that at a slow pace (up a hill, for example) at 2 kilometres per hour it will take you 30 minutes to walk 1 kilometre. At an average walking pace of 4 kilometres per hour it will take 15 minutes to walk 1 kilometre. If you're undertaking a long expedition you will need to remember to look for campsites, take account of the terrain (mountains, deserts, swamps etc.) and you will need to work out how much food, water and equipment to take.

How to Catch Giant Anacondas

The longest land animals alive, giant snakes are either boas or pythons. Boas bear live young, whereas pythons lay eggs. Giant snakes are not venomous. They are constrictors, meaning they catch and squeeze their prey to death.

Top 6 Giant Snakes

1. Anaconda

Giant anacondas like to hang out in rivers and are the largest (i.e. biggest and heaviest overall) snakes in the world. Found in tropical South America, they may reach lengths of 9 metres or more, measure 30 cm in diameter and weigh a quarter of a tonne!

2. Reticulated Python

The reticulated python of Southeast Asia is the longest snake in the world. The record length for this species is 10 metres!

3. African Python

The largest snake in Africa, African pythons can be found south of the Sahara Desert and may grow more than 6 metres long.

4. Indian Python

Similar in size to the African python, Indian pythons are found in India, Pakistan, Sri Lanka. southern China and Indonesia and may grow more than 6 metres long, but most average 4 metres.

5. Amethystine Python

The amethystine python lives in Australia, Indonesia, Papua New Guinea and the Philippines. It may grow more than 7 metres long but the average size is about 3–4 metres. The amethystine python is the thinnest of the giant snakes and is unable to kill large animals.

6. Boa Constrictor

With an average length of about 3 metres, the boa constrictor is the smallest of the giant snakes. They can be found in Mexico, Central and South America.

Fortune and Glory

You can claim a $50,000 reward from the Wildlife Conservation Society if you can catch a snake that is at least 9.144 metres (30 feet) long. It should be delivered alive and well with all necessary legal permits to the Bronx Zoo in New York City.

Prehistoric monster snakes

The *titanoboa* is the largest snake ever discovered. It lived 60–58 million years ago and fossils of this mammoth snake have been found in the coalmines of Colombia. It has been estimated the snakes grew up to 15 metres long, were 1 metre in diameter and weighted more than a tonne.

Amazing encounters

* In 1907 British explorer Percy Harrison Fawcett claimed to have shot a giant anaconda in the Amazon River measuring 19 metres.
* In 1959, a Belgian helicopter pilot named Remy Van Lierde photographed a giant snake on the ground in the Congo. It reared up threateningly as if to strike at the helicopter. The snake was estimated at about 12 or 15 metres in length. Assuming the story is true this must have been an African python as it is the only giant snake in Africa.

Catching giant snakes

Catching giant snakes is extremely dangerous. You will need an experienced team of people: 1 person for every metre of snake. For a powerful 9 m snake you will need 9 people.

Once a snake is spotted, an experienced member of the team will need to grab the neck just behind the head before the snake is able to strike and inflict a vicious bite. The rest of the team should spread out along the snake's length to support the body, tire it out and stop it crushing the person holding the head.

With someone holding the jaws closed, one of the team should tape the jaws shut and a 'blindfold' (a large cotton sock) should be placed over the head and taped around the neck behind the head. Tape should then be wrapped around the snake's jaws.

If any member of the team is bitten they will need immediate medical attention, and if the snake manages to wrap itself around anyone it should be immediately 'uncoiled', starting from the tail.

Once the snake is subdued it can be measured to check it is 9.144 metres (30–feet). This is notoriously difficult because snakes coil up and resist being straightened. The best way is to measure the body with string.

How to Deal with Mongolian Death Worms

You are leading an expedition searching for rare dinosaur eggs in the Southern Gobi Desert. Suddenly, a member of your team shouts 'Death Worm!' As the expedition team leader, you must take charge of the situation.

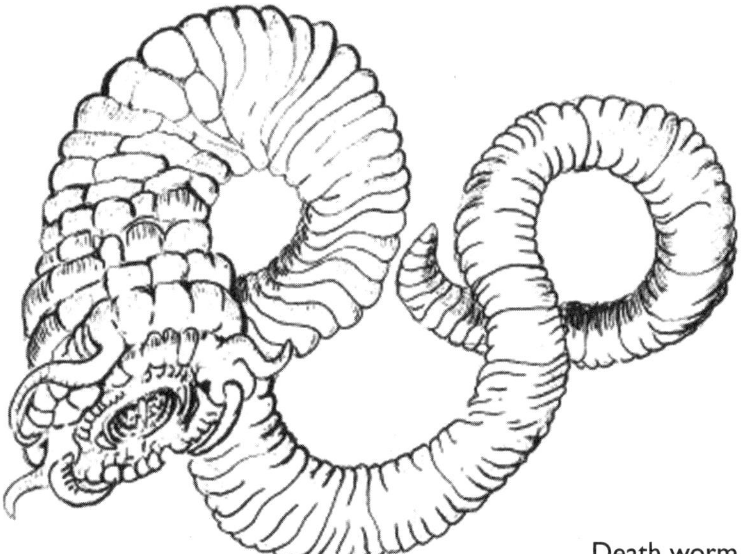

Death worm

How to recognise Death–Worms

The Mongolian Death–Worm or *allghoi khorkhoi* is a legendary half metre long blood–red worm that looks like a slithering cow's intestine and lives in the Southern Gobi Desert of Mongolia. You are most likely to encounter a Mongolian Death Worm in the hot months of June and July after rain. A number of expeditions have tried finding the worm, but no one has managed to produce conclusive proof of the worms' existence. Most of the information available about death worms comes from the accounts of local people. In summary, the dangers are as follows:

* The Mongolian Death Worm inflates itself and squirts acid–like venom at unfortunate victims causing burns and possibly death.

* The Death Worm can cause death at a distance of several feet by electrocution.

* To touch a Death Worm means instant death.

Dealing with death worms

1. We can understand Death Worm behaviour by comparing them to spitting cobras and electric eels. Spitting cobras only spit venom in self–defence. Assume that the Mongolian Death Worm also spits in self–defence i.e. when it feels threatened. Goggles or sunglasses and long–sleeved clothing may offer some protection, but the key is to BACK OFF and give the creature plenty of space. NEVER try to touch a death worm.

2. Electric eels discharge electric shocks in water to stun prey. The death worm probably does the same on land. To avoid electrocution by a Death Worm wear rubber–soled boots and never prod the ground with metal poles or poles made of other electricity–conducting material.

3. Special care should be taken in the months of June and July, especially after rain. Be sure to brief your team on the dangers.

4. Some reports suggest the Death Worm is associated with the saxaul plant. Learn to recognise them.

How to Use Walkie Talkies

Walkie–talkies will help you keep in touch with fellow monster hunters. However, if you don't know how to use them properly, communication can be difficult and a vital message could be lost.

Before you set off

Make sure your team's walkie–talkies are all tuned to the same channel. Each member of the team should then do a 'radio check' to make sure their walkie–talkies are working. Everyone should speak into their walkie–talkie and say 'radio check' (not all at the same time!). Anyone hearing should answer by saying 'check good'.

Call signs

Assign each member of the team a simple call sign e.g. Ranger 1, Ranger 2, Ranger 3 etc.

Learn the lingo

Make sure your team are familiar with the following radio terms.

Affirmative	Yes
Negative	No
Understood	I Understand
What is your 20	What's your location?
Correction	I made a mistake, I meant to say...
Do you read / copy	Please reply to my message
Go ahead	I'm listening
Roger	Message received
Over	I've finished speaking, you may want to come back to me
Out	My message has ended, I don't expect a reply
Say again	Repeat the last message
Stand by	I'm busy, wait a moment
Wilco	Message understood, I will follow the instructions
ETA	Estimated time of arrival

The Phonetic Alphabet

The phonetic alphabet has been constructed in such a way that letters have a distinctive sound to avoid any confusion. Use it to spell out important words or when you have poor reception due to static.

A	Alpha
B	Bravo
C	Charlie
D	Delta
E	Echo
F	Foxtrot
G	Golf
H	Hotel
I	India
J	Juliet
K	Kilo
L	Lima
M	Mike
N	November
O	Oscar
P	Papa
Q	Quebec
R	Romeo
S	Sierra
T	Tango
U	Uniform
V	Victor
W	Whisky
X	X–Ray
Y	Yankee
Z	Zulu

Pronunciation of numbers:

0	Zero
1	Wun
2	Too
3	Thuh–ree
4	Fo–wer
5	Fi–yiv
6	Six
7	Seven
8	Ait
9	Niner

How to Escape from Man–eating Trees

You have probably heard about venus flytraps, carnivorous little plants that trap and 'eat' insects and make fascinating 'pets'. But what about trees capable of devouring dogs, cattle and even people? Could such trees exist?

As yet, no one has managed to collect a specimen. If you think you're up to the job, here's where to look and how to survive.

Man-eating tree

The Land of the Man–eating Trees

Mysterious Madagascar is an island off the south east coast of Africa. The fourth largest island in the world, Madagascar is home to an incredible range of plants and animals, many of which are found nowhere else on the planet. It would seem to be a good place to find a man–eating tree.

In 1878 Polish biologist Dr Omelius Fredlowski received a mysterious letter from a German adventurer called Carl Liche. Liche had been visiting a primitive Madagascan tribe, the Mkodos. While with the Mkodos he claimed to have witnessed the sacrifice of a native girl to a tree that looked like a giant 2.5 metre tall 'pineapple.'

The bark was dingy brown and 'as hard as iron'. From the top of the tree eight thorny leaves hung down to the ground and in the centre of the leaves was a hollow oozing with honey–sweet liquid. 'Long hairy green tendrils' surrounded the hollow and above these were six white 'palpi' (feelers) that 'reared themselves towards the sky, twirling and twisting with marvellous and incessant motion.'

After sinister 'prayers' the girl was surrounded by spear–wielding tribesmen and forced to climb the tree and drink the liquid. In Liche's words,

'The atrocious cannibal tree that had been so inert and dead came to a sudden savage life. The slender delicate palpi, with the fury of starved serpents, quivered a moment over her head, then fastened upon her in sudden coils round and round her neck and arms.'

The leaves closed around the victim and remained closed for ten days. Then, one morning, Liche found them open. All that remained of the girl was a white skull at the foot of the tree.

More Killer Trees

The Nicaraguan vampire tree

A vampire tree that can be found in the swamps around 8156 square kilometre Lake Nicaragua, the largest lake in Central America. A botanist hunting for plants heard his dog cry out and found the animal tangled in rope–like vines. When he cut the dog free it was covered in bloody spots.

Carnivorous trees of the Amazon

The devil or octopid tree is said to be native to Mato Grosso in south–central Brazil. It conceals its branches under the ground and ensnares anything that trips over them. It was within the vast, dense jungles of the Mato Grosso region that legendary British explorer colonel Percy Harrison Fawcett thought he would find an El Dorado–like lost city he called 'Z'. It is also the region in which he disappeared. The victim of a devil tree?

The Amazonian monkey trap tree likes to eat – you've guessed it – monkeys! It lures them to their doom with an irresistible scent. Once they climb up the trunk there is no return!

The Mexican snake tree

Found in the Sierra Madre Mountains, Mexico. Like the Nicaraguan vampire tree it has moveable snakelike vines with blood–draining suckers.

The Indian cowcatcher

A cow left to graze in an Indian forest was allegedly grabbed by a small 'carnivorous' tree and partly lifted off the ground. The incident happened in 2007 near the remote village of Patrame in a forested region near Uppinangady. Villagers hacked the tree to pieces and freed the animal. Locally cow–catching trees are known as a 'tiger trees', and an iron sickle is the recommended defence against attacks.

Dealing with man–eating Trees

What do you do if you're about to be gobbled up by a plant? Trees may take many months or even years to kill – time you don't have. Here are a few ideas that may show a man–eating tree you mean business:

* If grabbed, try to hack off the tendrils with your machete (you did remember your machete, didn't you?) Uncoil tendrils the same way as giant snakes: tail first (end of tendril first).

* If this doesn't work, remember the most vulnerable part of any tree is its roots. Roots are vitally important to trees. They draw water and nutrients to the tree and anchor it to the ground. If they are visible and you attack them the tree may release you.

* If this doesn't work target the most vulnerable part of the tree above the ground – the bark. An old method for killing a tree is called 'girdling' or 'ring barking' where a ring of bark is removed. The hard outer bark protects the tree from the elements, but the soft inner bark carries food to the living parts of the tree and may be vulnerable if you can get to it.

How to Choose a Base Camp

Here are some tips to help you choose the perfect location for your expedition base camp.

* Practice setting up and packing away your tent before you set out. Be sure to thoroughly test the tent by sleeping in it so you can be sure it is suitable for your expedition.

* In wild country allow several hours before nightfall to find a good expedition base camp.

* Choose a flat or gently sloping spot that is well drained, dry and sheltered from the prevailing wind. Pitch the tent so that the entrance is out of the wind, and remember to insert pegs securely at a slight angle away from the tent to make it more resistant to high winds.

* Never set up camp directly below steep ground due to the risk of rock falls and avalanches.

* Trees provide fuel for fires and shelter from winds, but make sure you don't camp to close to them due to the danger of dead trees falling and lightning strikes.

* Choose a site close to water but think carefully about the risk of flooding and the danger from wild animals. Valley bottoms, marshy areas and the inside bends of rivers should be avoided because they are prone to flooding.

* Be sure that any animals travelling to a river or lake to drink or leaving the water to feed (e.g. hippos) will not have to pass through your camp to get to and from the water. Look out for trails and tracks that could indicate danger and move to higher ground to get out of their way.

* If you set up an expedition camp in man–eating wild animal/deadly monster country you may want to build a high and thick 'boma' around the camp, made of thorny bushes and trees like acacia. You could also rig up an animal alarm system with string attached to empty tin cans filled with stones.

* Avoid sleeping at ground level in jungles – dangerous snakes and creepy crawlies will make your life a misery. Always check your boots for creepy crawlies like scorpions and spiders before putting them on.

* Site your fire away from the tent and downwind so smoke doesn't blow towards it.

* Your expedition 'toilet' (a hole in the ground, usually – at least 15 cm deep) should be downstream and downwind of the campsite, 50 metres away from your source of water to avoid contamination. Burn toilet paper (don't bury it) or better still use moss.

* The smell of food may attract wild animals like hyenas and bears. Keep food well covered and use an overhanging branch to suspend food bags 3-4 metres in the air with a rope, at least 1.2 metres from the trunk. Choose a tree well away from you tent, preferably downwind.

* Leave no trace of your expedition camp. Pack rubbish away, put rocks back in their original position and make sure fires are completely out and covered in such a way as to blend in with the surrounding soils or vegetation.

How to Deal with Alien–robot Monsters

Occasionally you might come across monsters that don't seem to fit into any of the categories covered in this book: alien–robots with a sinister streak.

Take the Flatwoods Monster, for example. On September 12, 1952 a UFO was seen to 'crash' on a farm in Braxton County, West Virginia. A group of boys playing football decided to investigate. In some woods a hovering green creature with glowing eyes confronted them. A pointed hood or helmet covered its face and it had hands like grappling hooks. They fled in terror.

Sceptics have claimed the boys merely saw a 'frightening owl,' but whatever attacked Scottish forester Bob Taylor on November 9, 1979 it certainly wasn't an owl.

Bob and his red–setter dog were alone in a forest on Dechmont Hill when he became aware of an odd smell like 'chemicals'. Bob approached a clearing in the forest to investigate. His normally placid dog began to bark furiously, and it was then that Bob saw an object like a 'spacecraft'.

Suddenly a door opened then two 'robots' emerged. According to Bob they looked like, 'naval mines'. Slowly, the robots advanced and grabbed Bob by his trousers, ripping them and scratching his legs. They were trying to pull him towards the craft! He tried to fight them off and eventually awoke to find that the robots and the craft had vanished.

Police later sealed off the hill and found strange marks in the clearing: deep triangular marks and parallel caterpillar tracks.

Battling alien robots

So what can you do if you bump into a robot from another world? Here are some tips to get you out of a tight spot.

1. Run away in an unpredictable zig zag. Lumbering mechanical devices will have trouble computing your next move and reports

suggest people who become 'frozen with terror' have the most unpleasant experiences.

2. Don't try to match the strength of alien–robot–monsters. You'll be dragged away or beaten to a pulp.

3. If you see a button, press it. OK, you may inadvertently engage a 'self destruct sequence' but this is an emergency. If you're lucky, it might just be an off button. Look for strange writing like Egyptian Hieroglyphics.

Mammoth

How to Deal with Mammoths

You are investigating reports from hunters and local tribesmen who claim to have seen small, isolated herds of 'hairy elephants' in deepest Siberia.

Here are some helpful facts and essential safety tips:

Mammoth Facts

* Most mammoths died–out at the end of the last Ice Age, about 10,000 years ago. However, a small population of dwarf mammoths managed to exist on St Paul Island, Alaska until 8000 years ago and on Wrangel Island in the Russian Arctic until as recently as 4000 years ago.
* Although they are closely related, mammoths were not the ancestors of modern elephants. Elephants and mammoths descend from the same early ancestor species but have evolved separately. Think of them as 'cousins'.
* The reason for the complete disappearance of mammoths is something of a mystery. Hunting by humans and a period of climate change are top suspects.
* There are thought to be millions of mammoths frozen in the permafrost of Siberia.
* Woolly mammoths had extremely long curved tusks up to 4.2 metres long and shaggy outer hair up to 50 cm long. They may have used their curved tusks for clearing snow to reach buried vegetation.
* Woolly mammoths stood about 2.7–3.4 metres at the shoulder – the same as modern Indian elephants, but not quite as tall as African elephants. Exceptional African elephants can grow to nearly 4 metres tall at the shoulder and weigh seven tons (almost as high as a double–decker bus and just as heavy).
* The North American imperial mammoth and the steppe mammoth (from whom woolly mammoths descended) were some of the biggest members of the mammoth family and reached heights of 4 metres or more at the shoulder.

* Frozen mammoth remains can still contain large amounts of deep red beef–like flesh. As soon as they are exposed to air they thaw out they begin to rot and giving off an unbearable stench. This doesn't put off wolves however, who are rumoured to feast on ancient mammoth flesh when the opportunity arises.

The 'Mammoths' of Nepal

If you want to hang with 'mammoths', visit Nepal. For years, the Tharu people in the remote Bardia region of western Nepal reported crop-raiding 'giant elephants'.

In 1992 an expedition led by intrepid British explorer Sir John Blashford-Snell braved charging tigers to find the beast. They eventually observed and photographed two bulls.

They were huge, with footprints 57.15 cm across and heights of more than 3.4 metres. Each had two large domes on their forehead, sloping backs and other 'prehistoric' features.

Mammoths that time forgot? No. Tested showed they were Asian elephants, *Elephas maximus*.

Dealing with mammoths

Treat mammoths like their living relatives, African and Asian elephants.

Warning Signs

* Give mammoths lots of space and watch out when there are small calves in the herd.
* Thrashing about, trumpeting and sniffing the air are some of the signs that it's time to leave!
* Lone mammoth bulls in particular will sometimes launch a mock charge as a warning. This is done with ears spread out and loud trumpeting. If you're confident, stand your ground. It will probably stop a short distance from you, then turn and slowly walk off. When it retreats, move away very slowly downwind.
* Bare in mind that mammoth cows are more likely to follow through with a charge or charge without warning.

Attack!

A real charge can be recognised by ears flattened against the body and the trunk curled in. You won't be able to outrun a mammoth and if you climb a tree it may still get you. Mammoths are so big they can push trees over and can stand on their hind legs to reach up for you with their trunks. Your best bet is to run as fast as you can (downwind) and move quickly to one side just as it's about to crush you.

How to Spot Batman

Bat Facts:

- There are around 1000 known species of bat and they are divided into two main groups: mega bats and micro bats. Mega bats are medium to large bats with good eyesight and a strong sense of smell. Only a few members of this group echolocate (use ultrasonic sounds that humans can't hear) to find food and navigate. Micro bats are mainly smaller bats with small eyes that use echolocation to find food and navigate.
- The three known species of vampire bats are very small (micro bats). Only one type will happily suck your blood: the common vampire bat, since the other two prefer to feed on bird blood. The common vampire bat has a wingspan of 20 cm and is found in Mexico, Central and South America. The main danger from vampire bats is catching a nasty disease like rabies.
- Fruit bats or flying foxes can look like giant bat–winged monsters, particularly if you saw one at dusk. The world's largest bat is the rare giant golden–crowned flying fox of the Philippines. Its wingspan can exceed 1.5 metres.
- Look out for Africa's largest bat, the truly astonishing hammer headed fruit bat (Latin name *Hypsignathus monstrosus*). If ever a bat could be mistaken for a monster this is it! Males in particular have weird horse–like heads. Hammer–headed fruit bats live in equatorial Africa, especially in the Congo basin. They inhabit tropical forests, preferring wet areas near rivers and swamps, and are often found among mangroves and palm trees. Sightings of hammer headed bats may account for some bat monster reports in Africa.

Bat monster

Mystery bats

Giant vampire bats are not recognised by science. However, a strange tale from Africa hints that a blood sucking 'monster', unknown to science might await discovery. Eccentric explorer–archaeologist Byron de Prorok claimed he came across very large vampire bats with a 30–46 cm wingspan within 'The Devil's Cave' near a place called Lekempti, Ethiopia (note that de Prorok had a tendency to exaggerate, possibly to make his books more exciting).

Mystery bats larger than any previously recorded have been reported in jungles of Java and the Cameroon, Africa. The giant bat of Java is supposed to have a wingspan of up to 3.6 metres and can be recognised by its unmistakable call: 'A–hool'. The giant bat of Cameroon is known as the Olitiau. Famous naturalist and explorer Ivan T. Sanderson claimed he and companion Gerald Russell were attacked by an Olitiau with a 3.6 metre wingspan in the Assumbo Mountains in 1932.

Don't call Batman

The secret identity of Batman is, of course, Bruce Wayne. Or is it? Here are three bat–winged beasts you wouldn't want to call:

Mothman is a 1.8–2 metre tall humanoid with large black wings, little or no neck and glowing red eyes. A statue of the monster stands in the town of Point Pleasant, West Virginia, and a plaque reads, 'On a chilly, fall night in November 1966, two young couples drove into the TNT area north of Point Pleasant, West Virginia, when they realised they were not alone.' The spooky woods around the TNT factory (an abandoned ammunition works) became notorious for sightings. Some thought that Mothman was simply a large owl. However, on one occasion Mothman chased a car travelling at over 160 kph – something owls don't do!

Batsquatch is a cave–dwelling flying giant most often seen on 2550 metre Mount St Helens, Washington State and 4322 metre Mount Shasta, California. It is described as purple with the head of a bat, red eyes and the giant wings of a pterosaur.

The Orang–Bati ('winged men') of Indonesia are reported to be 1.5 metres tall, with red skin, a long tail and black leathery wings. Locals greatly fear the creatures that are said to attack children and carry them of to be devoured in the caves of an extinct volcano called Mount Kaiatu. US Marines near Da Nang, Vietnam saw a similar creature in 1969. As 'she' (the witnesses described the creature as a 'woman') flew over them they heard the sound of giant wings flapping in the warm night air.

RANGER TIP: A basic 'bat detector' will enable you to hear the ultrasonic sounds that bats make. With practice, you will be able to identify different species by their frequency range. Whether bat detectors can detect bat monsters is, of course, something you will have to find out for yourself! You can also have great fun spotting bats with a torch as they swoop down low over water when hunting for insects in the summer months.

How to Deal with Komodo Dragons

Warning! DO NOT read this if you are:

* **Easily upset**
* **Prone to nightmares**
* **Have a weak stomach**

The Komodo dragon is the world's largest lizard, an ancient species whose ancestors date back over 100 million years. Today is it only found on a few volcanic Islands in eastern Indonesia: Komodo, Rintja, Padar, and Flores. The Komodo dragon wasn't known to the west until 1910. Komodo National Park was set up to conserve the dangerous beast – the 'real' *Jurassic Park*. The largest recorded specimen was 3.13 metres long. Adults can consume up to 80% of their body weight in one gorging.

Dragon Attack!

Please remember that Komodo Dragons are endangered animals that should be treasured and respected. Humans are not usually on the menu and their natural prey includes deer and buffalo. That said they are superb predators with shark–like serrated teeth and may make the most of an opportunity.

It is extremely rare, but humans have been attacked, killed and eaten by dragons.

* In 2007 Mansur an eight year old boy was killed when he went to answer the call of nature behind a bush near his home in Kampung Komodo. In broad daylight a dragon lunged from his hide–out and took a bite of the boy's stomach and chest.
* In February 2009 a park ranger needed more than 30 stitches after a Komodo dragon attacked him. The dragon managed to climb into a hut where 46–year–old Main was sitting at his desk. Main escaped through an open window while colleagues drove the beast away with sticks.

* In March 2009 31–year–old Muhamad Anwar fell out of a sugar apple tree on the island of Komodo. Mr Anwar was left bleeding after being mauled by two waiting dragons. He died in hospital soon afterwards.

Dragon Survival Tips

* Komodo dragons are ambush predators. Even if an animal survives the initial attack, most bite victims die within a week. For years it was thought that dragons infect victims with dangerous bacteria found in their saliva. While their mouths are certainly disgusting, a team of top researchers found that dragons have a deadly secret weapon: venom. Dragon venom leads to reduced blood pressure, increased blood-loss and shock. Don't get bitten!

* Visitors to Komodo National Park should always be accompanied by a ranger and stick to trails. Rangers always carry a 'dragon staff' – a forked stick, 2.5 metres long. If a dragon becomes aggressive they use the Y–shaped end to push it away by the neck (this is highly effective, apparently). It can also be used as protection against snakes and other reptiles.

* If you find yourself alone in dragon country, make a dragon staff. Carry it at all times. Ward off inquisitive dragons by pushing their necks away with the Y–shaped bit. This stick can be used for walking and tracking monsters (see *How to Make A Monster Tracking Stick*). This will usually do the trick, but if it doesn't, and you need to run away, be aware that dragons can briefly run at speeds of up to 20 kilometres per hour.

* Komodo Dragons are cold blooded. They are mainly active during warm daylight hours and their peak activity (danger) times are 6–10 am and 2–5 pm. Their night vision is thought to be poor. This doesn't mean you'll be safe at night, however, since they are sometimes active after dark.

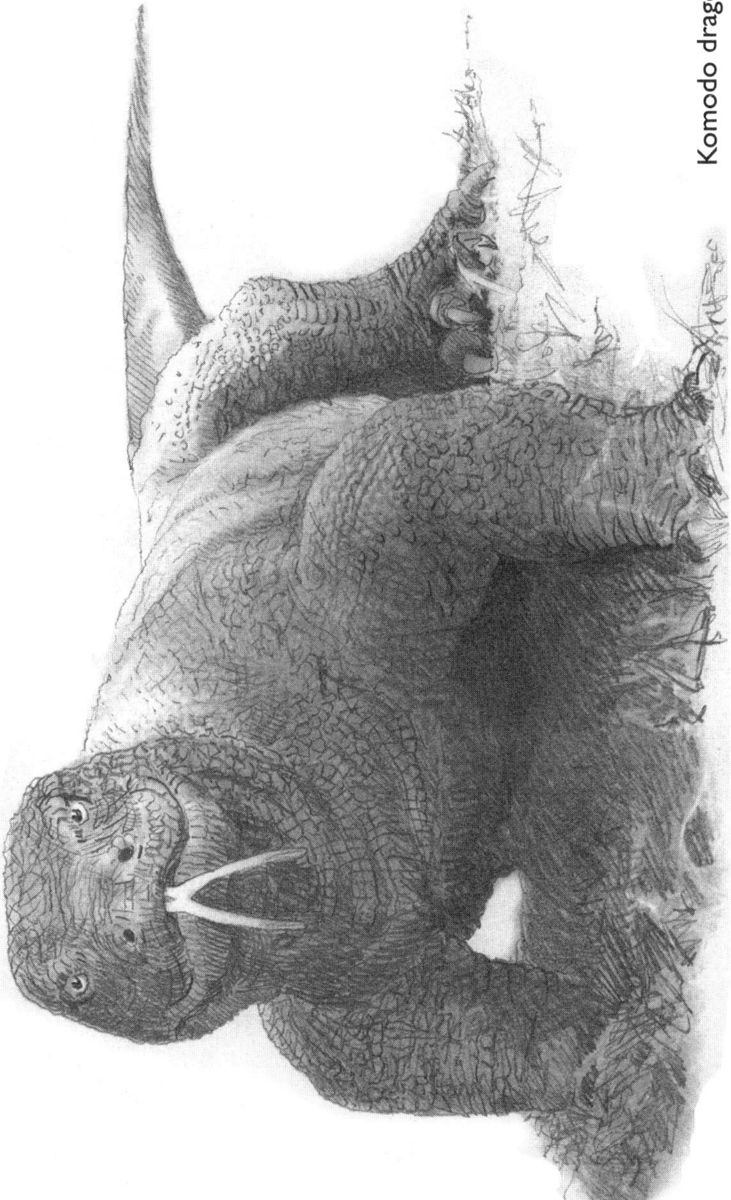

Komodo dragon

Dragon Survival Tips continued

* Komodo dragons ambush prey walking along game trails. Try to stay in open un–vegetated areas with good visibility like beaches to avoid a surprise ambush. Don't try to escape by getting into water. Komodo dragons are superb swimmers.

* Someone will need to keep watch at all times. Stay upright and avoid crouching.

* Komodo dragons have very sensitive noses. If you are really worried, you may have to resort to bashing the nose with your stick or even throwing stones. This is very much a last resort, but usually does the trick. In 2008 a group of divers became stranded on a beach in Rinca after 12 hours drifting in shark–infested waters. Exhausted and dehydrated, they fought off a Komodo dragon by pelting it with rocks until they were rescued. Fortunately for them, they didn't venture into the long grass and stayed on the beach where they could ward off the beasts.

* Noise and movement will attract dragons. Stay still and move as little as possible

* The scent of food and waste will also attract dragons. They can 'taste' the air with their flicking tongues and can track down potential meals up to a mile away!

Where to Track Dinosaurs

North American Tracksites

Dinosaur tracksites can be found throughout the world, but the most famous (and spectacular) are found in North America:

Colorado, The Picketwire Canyonlands Dinosaur Trackways, near La Junta,

Dinosaur track types: Theropods and ornithopods.

Notes: This remote and spectacular tracksite is one of North America's largest with around 1300 dinosaur tracks in 100 separate trackways.

Connecticut, Dinosaur State Park and Arboretum,

Dinosaur track types: Theropods.

Notes: 2000 dinosaur tracks were accidentally discovered during the construction of a new building. Around 500 tracks are on display under an enclosed dome.

New Mexico, Clayton Lake State Park,

Dinosaur track types: Mostly ornithopods with a few theropods and some ancient crocodiles.

Notes: An important and impressive outdoor track site with more than 500 tracks.

Texas, Dinosaur Valley State Park,

Dinosaur track types: Theropods, ornithopods and sauropods.

Notes: Has some of the best–preserved dinosaur tracks in the world, with a number of outdoor track viewing areas. Contains a possible theropod–sauropod 'chase scene'.

Utah, St. George Dinosaur Discovery Site at Johnson Farm,

Dinosaur track types: Theropods, sauropods and possible ornithopods.

Notes: An astounding tracksite, discovered in 2000. Many tracks are 3D 'casts'. In some of the casts actual skin impressions and claws are visible.

UK & European Tracksites

Some of the best dinosaur tracksites in the UK are found in coastal locations. The most accessible sites are Hanover Point on the Isle of Wight, the stretch of coast between Fairlight and Hastings in East Sussex and Bendricks Rock near Sully, South Wales. Coastal tracksites can also be found south of Whitby, Yorkshire and on the Isle of Skye in Scotland. In some locations, you will also find ancient shark and crocodile teeth, dinosaur bones and other interesting fossils.

WARNING : Coastal sites can be extremely dangerous. Stay well away from the base of cliffs and make sure you know the tide times.

European tracksites include:

Dino–Park Munchehagen near Hannover, Germany

Lavini di Marco dinosaur tracksite near Rovereto, Italy

Lommiswil dinosaur tracksite, Switzerland

Galinha dinosaur tracksite near Fatima, Portugal, Algarve Coast

Los Coyos dinosaur tracksite in the Province of La Rioja, Spain

Finally, remember that many museums keep collections of dinosaur tracks and trackways, and could well be worth a visit.

You might find dinosaur tracks in mesozoic rocks;

Era	**Period**	**Millions of years ago**
Mesozoic	Cretaceous	144 – 65
(Age of reptiles)	Jurassic	206 – 144
	Triassic	248 – 206

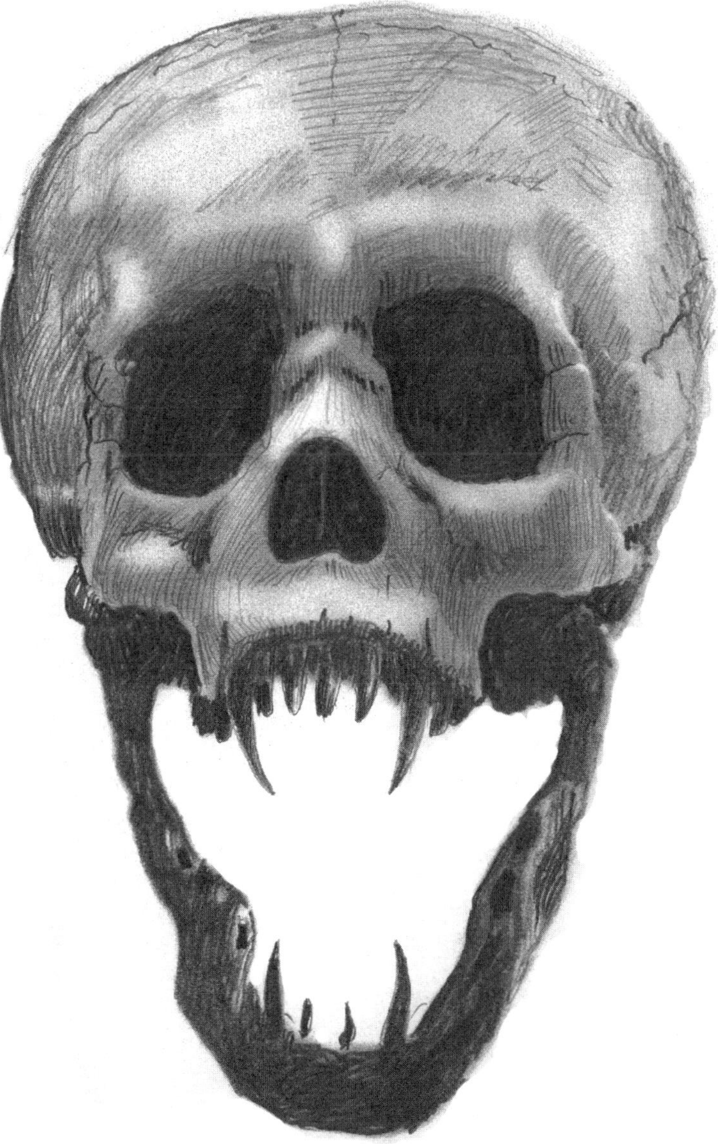

Yeti skull

First Aid for Beast Rangers

Wilderness adventures are not without risk. Accidents happen. This essential guide to first aid will help you deal with them.

Warning

This monster hunter's first aid guide should not be used as a substitute for professional training or a first aid manual. If in doubt, seek help

Common Problems

* **Minor cuts and scrapes**. Cuts and scrapes should be cleaned and covered with a plaster or appropriate-sized dressing.
* **Splinters**. Clean the area around the splinter and gently squeeze the surrounding skin to encourage the splinter out. Use tweezers to pull the splinter out the same way it went in. Clean and cover with a plaster. If a splinter is deep seek medical help.
* **Blisters**. On long treks friction from rubbing boots can cause blisters. Stop a blister forming by immediately covering tender spots with duct tape. Resist the urge to burst blisters because it makes infection more likely. If a blister is unbearable and you simply have to burst it, clean the area with soap and water. Pierce the edge of the blister with a needle thoroughly sterilised over a flame. Gently squeeze out the liquid and apply a sterile dressing. If a blister has already burst, wash with soap and water then cover with a sterile dressing.
* **Fainting**. Nervous members of your team may faint with surprise or fear when confronted by monsters. The person feeling faint should be made to lie down, their legs raised and their clothing loosened.

Animal bites

Animal bites can lead to dangerous infections, and in the case of a bite from a rabid animal rabies can be passed on to the victim.

Non-venomous animal bites should be thoroughly washed with clean water and soap or disinfectant then lightly bandaged.The victim should be given a prompt medical check-up..

If a victim is bleeding heavily apply a wound dressing and put pressure on the wound (preferably wearing gloves). If the dressing becomes soaked with blood do not remove the dressing as this could lead to more bleeding. Instead, apply a clean dressing on top and continue to apply pressure. Call for medical help.

Venomous animals

The spitting cobra (*Naja ashei*) and the legendary Mongolian Death Worm spit venom when provoked or surprised.Venom must be washed out of eyes with water or some other harmless liquid as it can cause blindness.The victim will require immediate medical help.

Wear high boots, long trousers and tread carefully where venomous snakes are expected. First aid treatment for snakebites requires identification of the particular snake species because the venom effect varies between species. Incorrect first aid treatment may have fatal consequences.

It is VITAL that the victim receives immediate medical treatment. Keep the victim calm and reassured and the bitten part of the body still.Try to memorise the snake's size, shape and colour (or take a photo if you have a camera and it is safe to do so). DO NOT attempt to catch or kill the snake, apply a tourniquet, suck the venom out of the wound or cut it with a knife.

Jellyfish

Jellyfish stings

The box jellyfish can be found in tropical and subtropical waters. It is one of the scariest creatures in the ocean. Box jellyfish venom is more powerful than that of cobras and can result in cardiac arrest within minutes. Victims report overwhelming pain and some don't make it back to shore alive.

General treatment for jellyfish stings

1. Prevention is better than cure. Stay alert in the summer, particularly on tropical beaches. In high-risk areas stay within sight of lifeguards and swim within special enclosures, if provided.

2. Never attempt to handle a jellyfish, even a dead one.

3. Don't make it worse. Don't rub the affected area with sand or anything else. Thoroughly rinse the area with salt water (don't use freshwater or urine). Careful pick away remaining tentacles with the edge of a shell or some other flat-edged object.

4. Vinegar is your best bet. Tiny stingers called nematocysts can be found at the ends of jellyfish tentacles. If tentacles are stuck to your skin nematocysts may continue to fire. Vinegar can disable some of the stinging cells if applied quickly and for at least 30 seconds. **Vinegar should not be used to treat Portuguese man-of-war stings**.

5. Jellyfish stings can be painful. An ice pack is the recommended for pain control.

6. If the victim has been stung by a dangerous species, in a sensitive area like the mouth or groin, is very young or old or shows signs of illness (nausea, vomiting, breathing difficulties, chest pain etc), call for immediate medical help.

Vampire avoidance

* Human vampires can be repelled with salt, garlic, crucifixes and holy water. Vampire beasts are more of a problem. By far the worst-case scenario is an attack by the three-toed reptilian vampire-beast of Puerto Rico, Mexico and the southern United States known as El Chupacabra or 'goat sucker'. Reports suggest the victim is completely drained of blood, via two unmistakable pencil-sized puncture marks to the jugular vein. First aid is useless.

* Fortunately, the Chupacabra prefers goat, sheep and dog blood and hasn't yet turned its attention to humans (though it would be unwise to camp outdoors during a Chupacabra killing spree).

* For the adventurous Beast Ranger, problem bloodsuckers are more likely to include vampire bats, leeches, ticks and mosquitoes.

Vampire bats

* Vampire bats sneak up on their victims at night and slice through their skin with tiny blade-like teeth. The victim is injected with an anticoagulant (a substance that stops blood clotting so it runs freely). The bat laps at the blood like a cat drinking milk.

* Bites in humans are likely to be on fingers or toes where blood flows easily (especially the big toe). The bite itself is not dangerous, but the danger of contracting rabies means vampire victims should seek immediate medical advice.

Spider Bites

* Black widow spider bites should not be fatal to healthy adults, but may be dangerous for the young and old. Reassure the victim and clean the bite with soap and water. Apply an ice pack or a bag of frozen peas wrapped in a towel for brief periods. If possible trap or kill the spider for identification (taking care not to get bitten) or keep the spider if it is already dead. Call for medical help.
* Sydney funnel-web venom is highly toxic and fast acting. Bite victims require immediate medical help. If possible trap or kill the spider for identification (take extreme care not to get bitten), or keep the spider if it is already dead. Bites should be firmly bandaged to slow the spread of the venom, starting at the bite site; working up the limb until the entire limb is covered. Keep the limb still (a splint is recommended) and the victim calm.
* Brazilian wandering spider venom is also highly toxic and fast acting. Again, correct identification of the spider could be lifesaving. Call for immediate medical help; keep the bitten limb still and the victim calm.

Leech attack!

Watch out for leeches when travelling through tropical jungles and swamps. Most leeches are small, but a few grow to worrying sizes. The world's largest, the giant Amazon leech (*Haementaria ghilianii*), for example, can grow up to half a metre long!

Don't be tempted burn a leech, use salt or pull it off as it may regurgitate into the wound and make the problem worse.

To remove a leech:

1. Look for the oral sucker at the narrow end of the leech.

2. Put your finger on your skin next to it and firmly slide the sucker sideways, using your fingernail.

3. When the oral sucker is dislodged, quickly do the same to the sucker at the fat (rear) end and flick the leech away.

4. Clean the wound with soapy water then apply a dressing. The wound will itch but this is perfectly normal.

A leech that gets into the nose, ear or throat could be dangerous as it expands with blood, so immediate medical help should be sought. In an extreme emergency 'pop' leeches with a sharp object or get the victim to gargle a strong alcoholic drink.

If you ever find a leech attached to your EYEBALL do not attempt to remove it as your eye could be damaged. Wait until the leech finishes its feast and drops off naturally. This will be an extremely unpleasant experience, but there really isn't much else that you can do.

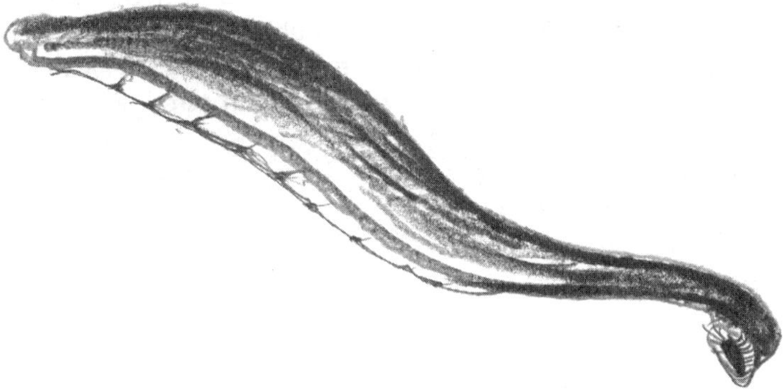

Leech before feeding

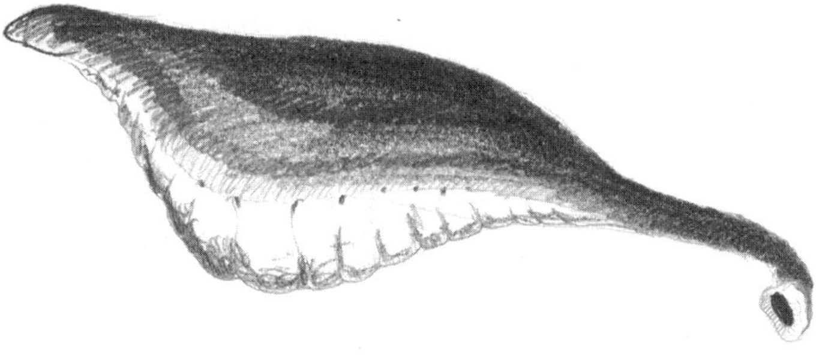

Leech after feeding

Tick Tips

These tiny bloodsucking relatives of spiders can pass on nasty diseases like Lyme disease and should be removed as soon as they are detected. To remove a tick, grasp it with fine-tipped tweezers as close to the skin as possible and steadily pull upwards. Do not attempt to twist the tick when using tweezers as it may regurgitate into the wound. If the victim develops a 'bulls eye' rash spreading from the bite site or feels ill 3-30 days after a bite they should seek medical advice.

Mosquito menace

* Mosquitoes are by far the deadliest bloodsuckers on planet Earth, responsible for more human deaths than any other animal. The actual bite from a mosquito may be irritating but rarely causes serious problems. In some countries, however, mosquitoes carry deadly diseases like malaria.

* Prevention is better than cure. Mosquitoes are mainly active between dusk and dawn. When in mosquito country use insect repellents, cover exposed skin and sleep under a mosquito net.

RANGER TIP: If your mobile phone doesn't work you can signal for help in the wilderness with a whistle (give three blasts in succession and repeat), by using a mirror to reflect sunlight or by lighting three fires, set in a triangle about 30 metres apart. To send an SOS signal with a torch the correct sequence is three short flashes followed by three long flashes followed by three short flashes.

Tasmanian tiger (Thylacine)